PRAISE FOR

Complete KOBOLD Guide to Game Design

"A must-have book for both those looking to get into this industry, and those who merely want to play."
—NerdTrek.com

"Highly recommended for gaming nerds everywhere."
—citybookreview.com

Winner, 2012 Gold ENnie Award for Best RPG-Related Accessory

KOBOLD Guide to Worldbuilding

"Class is in session . . . The Kobold Guide to Worldbuilding SHOULD be considered a textbook on intelligent setting creation."
—Dave Hinojosa, The Gaming Gang

"While the book is aimed at the RPG crowd, a huge percentage of the material would be just as valuable to an author writing a novel set in an original world. . . . The Kobold Guide to Worldbuilding will spark some new ideas and help you add the proper doses of verisimilitude and outlandishness."
—Ed Grabianowski, i09

"A really great work ... if you're seriously pursuing worldbuilding as a hobby, I think it's a worthy investment."
—Martin Kallies, RPG.net

Winner, 2013 Gold ENnie Award for Best RPG-Related Accessory
Winner, 2013 Gold ENnie Award for Best Writing

OTHER BOOKS IN THE AWARD-WINNING KOBOLD GUIDE SERIES

Complete Kobold Guide to Game Design

Kobold Guide to Board Game Design

Kobold Guide to Worldbuilding

Kobold Guide to Magic

Kobold Guide to Combat

Find all Kobold Press titles at
www.koboldpress.com

KOBOLD GUIDE TO PLOTS AND CAMPAIGNS

With essays by

James Jacobs

Jeff Grubb

Wolfgang Baur

Robert J. Schwalb

Steve Winter

Clinton J. Boomer

Kevin Kulp

Margaret Weis

Ree Soesbee

Richard Pett

Ben McFarland

Zeb Cook

Amber E. Scott

Edited by Michele Carter

KOBOLD Guide to Plots and Campaigns
© 2016 Open Design

Editor Michele Carter
Cover art Marcel Mercado
Interior art Tyler Walpole
Publisher Wolfgang Baur
Accountant Shelly Baur
Art director/graphic designer Marc Radle

OPEN DESIGN
P.O. Box 2811
Kirkland, WA 98083

WWW.KOBOLDPRESS.COM

First Edition

TABLE OF CONTENTS

Kobold Guide to Plots and Campaigns

BEGINNING A CAMPAIGN

James Jacobs

S o however it's happened—a burning drive to tell a story, a lost bet or subversive dare, a passion to entertain and create, or simply because it's your turn among your friends—the time has come for you to take on the role as Gamemaster for your group. It's time for you to start your next campaign.

Regardless of the setting you choose or the system you favor, not much compares in gaming to the excitement and wonder of sitting down at the table for the first session of a new campaign as a player. You've created your fresh new character. Maybe you have a custom-painted miniature, wrote up a 3,000 word backstory, or commissioned or created artwork to show off the new arrival to your friends. Or perhaps you've arrived at the table with a pregenerated character after a long day of work and are simply looking forward to a good time with good friends. Either way, you've got your character, your dice, and an appetite for roleplaying; you're ready to go!

But if you're the GM, it's not that simple. We'll assume that you've already handled all the complexities of building and preparing to run your game, from writing or selecting the adventures to deciding on the overall plot—the rest of the essays in this book give great advice on how to accomplish these goals. But what happens at that first session at the table in play will, in large part, set the theme for the entire campaign. As such, your first session of a new campaign is perhaps the most important session of them all. To start your campaign with a splash, consider taking the following steps.

BEFORE THE FIRST SESSION

It can be tempting to keep everything about your campaign a secret from your players. After all, you've likely got lots of twists and turns planned for the next few weeks or months of play, and you don't want to spoil the wonder of those surprises for your players. Further, it's easy to fall into the trap of thinking that just as we don't know what tomorrow might bring and thus can't plan accordingly, so must characters in an RPG be prevented from being able to plan for the next day's adventure.

This is a false assumption—and potentially a mistake that can hold back the fun of your campaign. In the real world, we might not know what surprises life has in store for us tomorrow, next week, or in ten years, but we still generally know what to expect from the world. When you start a new campaign, your players represent characters who grew up in a world that only you know. It can be easy to lose sight of this fact—after all, you might have spent months or even years building up the campaign and know it inside and out. This problem is lessened if this isn't the first campaign you've run in the setting you're using or if your game takes place in a published setting, but your players still need to understand the baseline assumptions. You are their window into the world you're creating, and until you tell them that "sunlight causes madness so no one goes out until it's dark," or "elves in this game have three eyes and can observe emotional states as visible auras," or "the most popular deity among humanity recently died and this game is set in the city where he was supposed to manifest," your players have no idea what their characters are getting into.

Think of your campaign not as a surprise party but as a big movie event, one that everyone at your table wants to attend because they all saw the preview for the movie and are excited by what they saw. Movie previews are called "teasers" for a reason—they tease you with something interesting, but don't give you the whole story. You're given barely enough information to be intrigued: "Why was the Statue of Liberty's head rolling down the street?" or "What was at the other end of that claw reaching out of the sewer grate?" are much better ways to persuade someone to go see a movie than simply relating a title that might not have any obvious bearing on the movie's contents. Even a mysterious or confusing title is better than expecting someone will want to spend two hours of their life watching a movie they know absolutely nothing about other than the fact that you want them to watch it with you. You need to sell the campaign to your players a little bit, working on their curiosity and building excitement.

NAMES AND TEASERS

That isn't to say titles aren't important. You'll definitely want to settle on a name for your campaign as early as possible. The right name can serve as a teaser all on its own, but the best titles use words that your players know and understand. If your campaign is a political drama set in the fantasy city of Bezmalar where a reincarnated dragon is getting up to no good, but no one in your group has ever heard of Bezmalar, a title like "The Bezmalar Affair" is not only confusing but potentially misleading. Is "Bezmalar" a person? A place? A deity? A disease? Without context, that nonsense word is just that: nonsense. A better name for a campaign uses words that your players understand. Something like "Secrets of the Serpent Scion" or perhaps "Throne of Whispers" or even "Wrath of the Dragon's Ghost" can all work for a campaign like this. Don't be afraid of outright spoiling the nature of the big bad at the end; "Wrath of the Dragon's Ghost" lets your players know that the campaign will most likely involve a dragon, perhaps an undead one.

So when you announce to your players that you'll be starting a campaign, tease it. Tell them something about what they can expect: where it's located, what levels they can expect to reach, what kind of monsters and challenges they can generally expect to face, what sorts of allies and treasures they might gain, and what the main plot is about. You don't need to flat-out spoil everything; if you're running a campaign in which the main villain is a reincarnated soul of a world-eating dragon who has come back in this cycle as the queen who recently inherited the throne—a ruler who remembers her past life as a dragon and is destined to transform into that dragon for the final fight—well, you don't need to mention dragons at all in your teaser. It's enough for the characters to know that the queen has been acting strangely, and that word of a dragon cult has been rising in the shadows of the city, and perhaps that the two elements might be connected.

To convey a campaign's teaser to your players, you can simply describe it to them or send a brief description in an email. For Paizo's published Adventure Paths, we create "Player's Guides" that go into extensive detail about what sort of character options would be appropriate for the game (down to recommending what kind of enemies players should expect to face, or what sort of animal pets might be logical choices) and describe the region in which the campaign takes place (or at least starts in). Maps and artwork can serve to preview your campaign as well, and if you've got the skills and resources, you can even create a short video to share with your players as a teaser that uses art, maps, and music of your design or borrowed from online resources as appropriate. Even a single sheet of paper with relevant bullet points and art that suits the tone will encourage players to think along the right lines. As long as your players know what they're getting into, and as long as you see them get excited about what they're getting into, you're on the right track!

PREPARING FOR THE GAME

Of course, getting your players on board with playing in your campaign is only the start. The first session of your new campaign is in a lot of ways the most important one you'll run. Obviously, you want the last session of the campaign to be strong and memorable, but the unfortunate reality is that not all campaigns ever reach that last session; a lot can happen to throw even the best game off the tracks and end it before its time. This places even more importance on the campaign's first session, since if you don't hook the players with your game as strongly as you can with that first episode, chances of player attrition increase.

Beyond this, you want your first session to be memorable because it's going to set the theme and lay the foundation for every session to follow. First impressions count, and if you show up to run this initial game and are unprepared or uninspired, your players will be more likely to lose interest or find something else to do with their time when the second session rolls around.

To make your first session, and thus your entire campaign, as perfect as possible, you need to know your players as well as you know their characters. If you have copies of the PCs before you start the first session, you can adjust your campaign as appropriate to give them the best play experience. Early familiarity with the characters allows you to incorporate character backstories into the campaign, to give each PC a built-in story arc to pursue during the game. But it's just as important to understand your players: to know what interests them, what annoys them, and what their play styles are. If you're starting a new campaign with new players, you should strongly consider making the "first session" a character creation session and not plan on any actual gameplay. Order up some food and make a party out of making the party, so that you and the other players can get to know each other before you actually sit down and play.

Where you play is important as well. Preparing your game space for the first session not only helps make that initial game more memorable, but also sets expectations for the game going forward. Make sure there are no distractions, and if you want to include mood music or snacks or visual aids or other elements, take the time to set them up beforehand as well. Nothing grinds a game to a halt faster than spending 30 minutes fiddling with wireless speakers trying to get your mood music to work when you could be gaming! Once the campaign's under way, a session without all the bells and whistles is fine, but if you're including enhancements like this from the start, you want to make sure they work at the start!

THE FIRST SESSION

Before everyone's seated at the table and the game begins, consider the initial introduction. If you're running a published campaign, like one of Paizo's Adventure Paths or a regional adventure from Kobold Press, a fair amount of the setup work is already done for you. If you're building your own campaign, studying how published campaigns or starter adventures gather the characters together is time well spent for a GM. You can even borrow opening scenes from adventures you enjoyed playing or reading, manipulating and changing them as necessary to fit what you've planned.

During your first session, have the players introduce their characters. You can do this at the very start, or you can let the introductions occur organically in play, but it's important to give each player a few minutes to describe their character. As each PC is presented, you can help everyone remember all the new names. Have a whiteboard or a large sheet of paper on the wall for this step; you can also use markers on a battle mat or even pieces of paper folded like placeholders. Whatever your preference, note down each player's name—both for yourself as reference and for the other players. List the basic details of their characters as well—race, class, and gender, for example. As each player describes their character, ask them to give you a one or two word summary of that character's personality. This not only helps you and the other players get to know that PC more quickly, but also helps the player focus on a specific character trait in the first session that might well go on to define an entire campaign of personality choices.

The first encounter is equally as important as these first introductions. The classic (most would say "clichéd") opener to a fantasy-based RPG is the old and quite tired, "You all meet in a tavern." This trope works fine for quick games at conventions or even one-shot games where you don't intend to delve beyond the events of a single session, but the more you and your players have gamed, the less satisfying this framing device becomes. It's certainly not memorable.

START WITH DANGER, NOT MEALTIME

Rather than a passive, tired first scene, consider starting your campaign with a bang. The words "Roll for initiative" don't have to be the first out of your mouth as the game starts, but beginning with combat is a great way to catch your players' attention if they're not expecting an early fight. Of course, other dramatic events can stand in for the mayhem of combat. A tournament, a party, a festival, a shipwreck, or enduring a natural disaster all force the players to use their characters' skills and talents from the very start. It doesn't matter if the conflicts the PCs are resolving are small stakes (like who might win at a feat of strength at a county fair) or significant (whether they can move the caravan to high ground before the flash flood hits).

Keep in mind that you don't want to kill the PCs off in this very first scene! The chances of their success should be automatic, with skill checks and other rolls they make along the way simply determining the degree of success. Start a campaign out like an action movie: begin with a big set piece to get the audience excited and engaged. The James Bond movies have been using this technique for decades to great effect. You might even consider holding off on player character introductions until after this scene; after all, how a PC acts in a time of chaos and peril quickly defines a hero!

From this point on, the game should proceed as normal. Your players are hopefully hooked into your campaign and are eager to see where it goes. As the first session draws to a close, there's one more way you can make the campaign's beginning even more memorable: prizes! These don't have to be outlandish; gifting each player with a set of dice themed to your game is a cool way to thank them for taking part in the game. If you've the talent or funds to pull it off and have the time to plan in advance, paying for custom art or miniatures for their PCs can be a staggeringly creative way to invest your players in your game. But virtual prizes can be just as compelling. Handing each player a piece of paper with the words, "Fate is on your side. At any point during this campaign, you may turn this card in to the GM to avoid one certain death situation!" or something to that effect can help make your campaign's first session not only important and memorable . . . but one that your players will be glad to have not missed!

OTHER PEOPLE'S STORIES
Running Published Adventures

Jeff Grubb

I often use adventure modules when I'm running roleplaying games. There, I said it. I use adventures written by others rather than wracking my own brain to come up with new and exciting ways of challenging my players. Usually this is for my *Call of Cthulhu* games, but with the release of *5th Edition Dungeons & Dragons*, I have been using adventures written by others when I'm running *D&D* as well.

I know, this is a surprise. The idea that a published game designer would use a prewritten adventure seems akin to a master chef admitting that he uses canned soup, or that his favorite macaroni and cheese comes in a narrow blue box. But it is true, and this method has great advantages.

Mind you, I come from the great primeval days of the hobby when creating your own dungeons (heck, creating your own entire campaign worlds) was more of a necessity than an option. Back when the official adventures were the *GDQ* series, and everyone had played through THOSE, and no one would touch the now-classic *Tomb of Horrors* after it resulted in three straight Party Wipe-Outs (which is what us old folks called what you kids call TPKs). In that pre-Internet landscape there were good tournament adventures, but they were just that—one-shots or limited series.

These days, we have a lot more resources available to us. Forty-plus years of classic RPG adventures have made it a tad easier to pull something off the shelf for a quick night's gaming. The Internet groans with potential options, and perusing eBay and the local used bookstore can be extremely rewarding for tracking down original versions. And while roleplaying games go through frequent updates, revisions, and editions, the foundational work is generally solid enough that you can take older works and update with a minimum of fuss (though your mileage may vary).

Yet there is still the air of something amiss in this approach—the assumption that if you are not making your adventure biscuits from scratch, you're doing something wrong. So let me tell you why you should use other people's stories. Canned adventures. Adventure modules. Then let me tell you what you do with them.

THE CONVENIENCE OF OFF-THE-RACK ADVENTURES

First off, you should use adventure modules when you're pressed for time (and the older I get, the more pressed time seems to become, for some reason). Pulling something off the shelf and reviewing it the night before, making notes, and even introducing custom changes is generally easier than weaving an entire epic out of whole cloth. Adventure modules are a convenience that should be embraced.

Second, published adventures come with an inherent assumption that they've been played before. That's not always true, of course, so you should always check the ingredient list, and by that I mean the credits. Are there playtesters? How about thanks for a particular gaming group? Was it run as a tournament module, then expanded? Even a design reviewer is a good sign that *someone* other than the author and maybe the editor looked at the module as an adventure that would be run by other people.

Third, published adventures (good ones, at least), tend to anticipate the basic character actions in the game and help guide you on how to facilitate the game. No, it won't help you with dealing with your player who is running a bard and who challenges every opponent to a dance-off. But it will give you the basis for the defenses of an enemy encampment, or how the bandits will react if the players pull back after a few attacks. Handling the basics gives you more time to spend thinking about that dancing bard.

Fourth, published adventures have the advantage (generally) of professional production values. This is useful whenever you want to lay out a map in front of the players to show what the local town looks like, or how the inn is laid out. For games that rely on handouts (*Call of Cthulhu*, for example, makes great use of player handouts for newspaper clippings and excerpts from elder tomes), a higher level of professionalism helps sell the reality of the imagined world.

Finally and probably most important, adventure modules are like soup stock. They provide a foundation that you can build off of. Good adventure modules should give you—as the DM—ideas about what you can add and what you can do without, based on the needs of your players. Just like folks like their steak rare or their chili's spice turned up to eleven, your players have their preferences, and a good adventure module allows you to take what is presented and expand it to suit the table.

CHOOSE YOUR ADVENTURE . . . WISELY

I keep saying "good adventure module." What the heck do I mean by that? Ideally, it is an adventure that fits your needs, and both your DMing style and that of your players. Knowing the original intention of an adventure helps. Is it part of a larger series? Is it a one-shot? A killer dungeon? Something adapted from a tournament?

Let me stop on that last one for a moment.

Some of my earliest designs run for strangers were for the *AD&D* Open tournament at GenCon (back when it was in Kenosha, Wisconsin). These consisted of mostly straight-line adventures where the players would be judged on how far they got and how many characters they lost along the way, and had to be different for each session to keep from spoiling the adventures for the participants. By the same token, each adventure had to have a) a big melee, b) a small melee, c) a trap, d) a monster used in a new or different way, and e) a puzzle. The end results were adventures that worked very well for a tournament (and that I still haul out when I'm running at a convention), but not something that I would spring on a regular group (as they had a tendency to be decidedly fatal, since that was one of the measuring sticks).

So not only are we looking for something that has been run before, but also a bit of provenance. Knowing the origin of the adventure can aid in your decision-making. That last bit is not always easy to find, but sometimes designer notes tell you the history.

Now consider your players. What is their style of play? Some groups have a strong social element. Some want to kick the doors down and kill the monsters. Some want sit around and tell bad jokes (OK, admit it— you've done that), and see the dungeon as a straight man for their humor. The immortal *Tomb of Horrors* chewed through player characters at a time when PC life was cheap and easy. Running the same adventure with more established characters, who might have their own histories and stories and even coats-of-arms, would result in a lot of dead legends and possibly hurt feelings as well.

Another thing to consider is experience level. Not only of the characters (for those games that use levels) to determine the relative strengths of the encounters, but also of the players. Experience among the players is a real factor—are they wary in new situations? Do they know enough not to insult the king in that initial audience in his chambers? Do they tend to rush into combat, or have they concocted a general battle plan? Are they comfortable with the rules set? Knowing your audience is part of the trick as well.

Think about the length of the adventure, or the larger campaign that it is a part of. Is this something that you can set down neatly within your typical *Dungeons & Dragons* campaign without having to worry too much about gods and legends and lost empires? *Tomb of Horrors*, for all its lethality, is excellent for its portability. In its original form, as a dungeon delve located deep within a swamp, the adventure can be positioned pretty much anywhere without interfering with the workings of a larger campaign. The original *Ravenloft*, on the other hand, with all its excellent gothic trappings, needs a little more work to fit into a world of barbarians with mighty thews. As a result, it ended up in its own demiplane, which allows it to show up as needed without having to change the world around it.

ADAPTATION

I am part of a group that has been running *Call of Cthulhu* adventures for many years. Our group has no permanent Keeper (the GM in *CoC* terms), but rather shifts the responsibility between individuals. This works very well within *Call of Cthulhu*, since the adventures work best within a short timeframe. The game can be fairly lethal, both in terms of the characters' health and sanity. Also, the milieu can be applied to a number of different settings and timeframes; in one set of sessions you can be a group of clandestine agents of a modern conspiracy, the next you can be a group of students at Miskatonic University in the 1920s. This idea of a shifting Keeper works nicely to avoid burnout and allows the individual Keepers the chance to specialize in particular styles of gaming without tripping over each other.

In my case, I have been running a pulpy 1920's campaign based out of London. I like the historical nature of the era (the past is as much a fantastic universe as any dragon-ravaged imaginary kingdom). It is always 1928 in this campaign, and evil eldritch things lurk on the edges of the world.

My group is a grab-bag of *CoC* archetypes—the wealthy dilettante novelist and her adventurer companion who she writes about, the Chicago mobster on the run, the student archeologist, and the newspaperman/secret agent. They sorted out a rationale of how they have come together and formed a pretty tight group for dropping into adventures.

And these adventures have mostly (but not exclusively) been part of the *Age of Cthulhu* series from Goodman games, with a few inserted adventures from Cubicle 5. The Goodman series presents the pulp aspects of the game very well—exotic locations, secretive cults, and elder things pressing in on the walls of reality, which makes for the comfort food nature of the game.

The bulk of these adventures are plug-and-play. They usually include pregenerated characters, but the generally open nature of the introduction allows me to easily insert my merry band of comrades into the mystery at the start of the adventure. (And yes, I extensively use the "You receive a letter from an old friend asking for help, even though you know that by the time you get there, he'll be dead" excuse found in a lot of *CoC* adventures).

The adventures are short as well: playable over three sessions, four if we dawdle. And that fits the social nature of the group. The number of investigators tends to be greater than the adventures are designed for, which makes the fatalities fewer and the madness spread about more. But I tend to run it by the book, prepared to go haring off in unanticipated directions should the players suddenly get it in their heads that that the church basement obviously holds a clue to the Undying Cult they are chasing.

The chapter breakdown of such adventures, set in particular locations in the game and strung together with clues to move the characters from one place to another, makes for relatively pleasant running. While not a railroad, events must happen in a particular order, and it is not fully a sandbox adventure where the characters have all of London to roam through. Well, theoretically they do have all of London to roam through, but the plot won't advance until they reach that particular study in that particular old house with that particular secret passage leading down into the ghoul tunnels.

There was an exception in moving through the Goodman games series, and that was for a specific adventure built around the crash of the airship *Italia*, which had embarked on an exploration of the North Pole. For this one I asked the players to put aside their normal characters and instead create new ones that would likely be engaged in a rescue mission of the *Italia*. I did this because a) I could not see a traditional group of 1920s tropes, like itinerant jazzmen and hardnosed detectives, being involved in a polar rescue mission, and b) I didn't expect the characters to come back alive. (They did. Well, mostly.)

These adventures give me a foundation to research further, to get an idea of what Peru in the 20s was like or the history of an Indonesian port. We play in the age of the Internet, so a mention of a song inspires someone to pull up a YouTube video of it, and mention of a place results in someone calling it up on their iPad. Gaming in the modern age has to deal with players knowing more than they might otherwise, given that their characters would likely have that information.

My adventures tend to be run straight, with the GM keeping a hand on the rudder and seeing what the players bring to table with their characters, be they original or pregenerated, but other people's stories also can be reskinned for other use and personalization.

I am stealing the term reskinning from the computer games, where figures (heroes or monsters) are animated on a skeleton or rig. Often different exteriors or skins are placed on the same animation rig. So these reskins are adventures that have been more deeply adapted by the Keeper, which requires more investment but can create a deeper connection with the players.

Another member of my Cthulhu group is John Rateliff, a Tolkien Scholar and editor. John has run his own original adventures, but he also has adapted published material for the group. His adaptation of printed material is deeper than mine has been, in that he has moved encounters across the globe to create a more connected adventure.

John recently ran *The Walker in the Wastes*, an excellent adventure from Pagan Publishing by John H Crowe and Dennis Detwiller. The adventure shuttles all over the globe in dealing with a cult of an elder wind-god. John took this basis and rewired it, moving locations and times around to fit his needs. Our party began, not in Canada of the 20s, but in Alaska of the 1890s Gold Rush. He did this in part because he had already lifted the opening chapters of *Walker* for another game session he ran, and he did not want to repeat it.

So his initial adventure shifted 30 years into the past and several hundred miles to the west. The characters who survived that expedition reunited 30 years later in Seattle to continue the adventure. John kept some of the globe-girdling events in their original locations, but moved the material set in the Eastern U.S. to the Puget Sound region, as he was more comfortable with this region than East Coast. As a result, we encountered secret cult bases on Whidbey Island and dealt with the apparent connection between the town of Issaquah and the elder god Ithaqua.

The end result kept John as the Keeper on his toes, as he had to deal with, among other things, a time-traveling zeppelin run by refugees from the White Army that suddenly appeared in the narrative and then had to be dealt with. Yet our group hit all the plot points and resolved the adventure neatly in a fashion that was tailored first and foremost to the group.

LOOT AND PLUNDER

While I tend to run the adventure-as-written and John rewired the material but kept it basically intact, there is a third way to treat prewritten materials—as lootables. Written adventures have a lot of small bits that can easily be lifted and adapted to another area, even another genre, without too much difficulty.

For example, I was running the first adventure for *D&D* 5th edition, *Horde of the Dragon Queen* by Steve Winter and Wolfgang Baur, for a group of colleagues at work. Part of that adventure involves a long caravan trip, and, as opposed to having the characters camp out every night, I littered the route with waystops and walled inns. None were provided for this purpose in the adventure, but I had a lot of older *D&D* products with maps I could easily loot to provide reference.

Most of the time nothing was needed—the players were glad their characters had a place to crash that did not involve wolves howling in the distance and the night would pass without incident. But on occasion, when asked for the layout of the common room or the kitchen or if there was a way to sneak from their rooms without being seen, these pieces from other campaigns proved to be extremely useful.

And this can apply to larger campaigns as well. I mentioned how easily the original *Tomb of Horrors* can be slotted into any available swampland. Similarly, a host of self-contained lost tombs, ancient catacombs, wayside inns, and even towns can be ported directly over into large campaigns, providing spice to existing campaign or a strong basis for new ones. These can also provide side quests for ongoing campaigns, allowing a break from the epic nature of the overarching story, or light moments for characters to explore without continual fighting.

So adventures written by others have a firm place in the GM's toolbox. Not every biscuit needs to be made from scratch, and pregenerated, canned adventures can provide a time-saving tool, a foundation upon which additional work can expand, or a spice that can help an existing campaign. There is no sin in not reinventing the wheel, provided that the material is presented to the players in a new way and provides an impetus for greater adventure and storytelling.

CHOOSING AN ENDING FIRST

Plotting Backward to the Big Finale

Wolfgang Baur

Some campaigns or large adventures are episodic, wandering from dungeon to citadel to the Outer Planes without a clear story tying them together. That can be an absolute blast, with weekly episodes of heroic fun, and it's a popular play style because the installments stand on their own. However, I'd argue that the most popular and memorable campaigns are those that have a big finale, a huge finish, an earth-shattering ka-boom. It's certainly possible to create an epic ending on the fly, using your weekly plot notes (see Kevin Kulp's essay "Complex Plotting") to pick a direction, or going in a direction chosen by the players (see Zeb Cook on "The Art of Letting Go"). In many cases, though, episodic campaigns meander along from week to week with static, sitcom-style relationships that change relatively little; these are picaresque stories, where the delight is in the journey, not the destination. I'm talking here about campaigns where storylines resolve at a high level, and that's part of your plan as GM or designer from the start.

In these cases, the DM can also decide on the finale before the campaign or major adventure even starts—and this can produce very surprising, dramatic, memorable results. (Note, however, that even with this method, you need to retain flexibility—if you aren't careful to leave a little wiggle room, you might end up boxed in by your own plot.) This technique is one of the secrets used when developing written adventure paths and every save-the-world adventure scenario (whether the end-boss is Tiamat or Baphomet). It's a little less common in homebrew campaigns. Here are three steps to get you there.

EMPHASIZE YOUR WORLD

Aim for an ending that showcases something great about your particular world: its people, wars, magic, or particular threats and challenges. At the same time, the ending can change that element of your world in the way you want, to set up a future game or to make a certain impression.

Designing a finale specifically to a setting makes an ending stronger, because specific triumphs ("We beat the 33rd legion of the Dragon Empire! The Magdar ride for freedom!") always beats a generic triumph ("We beat the orc legion! Humans win!"). Consider the following options from the Midgard campaign setting:

- Characters prevent the triumph of the Dragon Empire and kill its emperor
- Characters meet the Shadow Court and lift its curse
- Characters restore the Bifrost bridge and bring about the return of the Elves
- Characters restore mana to the Wastes—or sound the death knell of magic
- Characters trigger Ragnarok and fight beside the Asgardians
- Characters destroy the Emerald Order and its dark god

Each of these options implies a certain type of campaign, whether heavy combat or investigation or apocalyptic. But each also shows off a particular element of the setting and has the depth to provide for months or even years of play. Choosing that finale first focuses your mind as a creator. A fight against the Dragon Empire means setting the game near the Empire, and through play showing its expansion and the destruction of neighboring states. Restoring mana to the Wastes likely requires a lot of investigation, special items, druidic lore, and tromping around a low-magic wilderness. Ragnarok is a great finale, and it also implies a Fimbulwinter and fighting a lot of giants.

What kind of adventure goal, and what aspects of your world, appeal to you most? You will get more out of it (and your players will too) if you think about the style of various types of endings. Great challenges, quiet success and retirement and a changed, better world? A twilight struggle against the most heinous demons? The death of a tyrant?

In other words, what sort of story does your world favor? What changes will come about from success? For me, if I have to pick something familiar, it's the often dark, brooding city-states, honest rebellions, fey meddling, and the rise or invasion of the undead. You probably have a sense of your favorite go-to themes—try one of those, or pick something you think your world can accommodate but that you've never attempted before.

Write down this theme, this style of story, and stick it somewhere you can see when working on the guts of the thing. Whether your chosen note card says "Demonic gang war massacre" or "Arcane College Duel to the Death," all other roads point to that.

CHOOSE AN ORGANIZATION TO OPPOSE AND FOIL PLAYERS

Another way to decide on an ending is to choose a villain worth defeating. Nazis are the classic go-to Hollywood villains for a reason: they're nasty, they have organization and a clear (terrible) purpose, and they come in a more-or-less infinite supply.

While it's possible to make a single villain the centerpiece of a long-running campaign, it's easier and more satisfying for the major foe to be a society, group, or cult of some kind. This group of linked characters shares a goal that your players hate. Maybe it's the hell knights of Asmodeus who plunder the kingdom as sea-pirates. Maybe it's a lich-king's undead barony that wants to conquer and enslave the living. Maybe it's just a zombie horde, but no one knows how to stop it. Maybe it's a circle of druids who want to expand the magic-dead zones of the world and restore the natural balance free of arcane meddling. Think about what your players dislike, and what their characters are going to truly despise. That's the organization you want. It needs to be vile, hideous, and frustrating, because the worse it is, the more motivated the characters will be to defeat it.

Just as important, this organization needs to be diverse in its power levels, its abilities, and its representatives. In other words, it needs to be interesting at 1st level and at 10th, and it needs to work as a foil for the players. To make it work, you need a hierarchy of villainy.

Everyone knows the ranking of mooks and minions as the least of foes, and end bosses as the major players. I think you should sketch out about four to five typical minions for your new organization, creatures that characters will meet many times. For a classic reptile cult, these might be goblins, lizardfolk, giant snakes, a set of minor snake demons, and human cultists.

The less-often discussed tier features what I call the sergeants. They boss the minions around, and they have individual plans or plots that they want to achieve. These goals are ideally related to the special elements of your world. A sergeant is a big boss of a little area; he commands resources, has allies, and knows secrets but he's not at the top of the villainous corporate hierarchy. While his or her defeat is certainly satisfying, it does not put an end to the villain's plans—it only deprives that ultimate villain of a very valuable servant. Think Ring-wraith, rather than Sauron.

THREE PLOT MILESTONES: WHAT TO VEIL AND WHEN TO REVEAL

Reverse-plotting your milestones is simpler than it might first appear. Three turning points can occur in rapid succession in a short campaign or over months in a longer one. These are discovery, reversal, and what I like to call the change in view.

Discovery

The discovery of the plot is step one, and it need not happen right away. The mere fact that the character don't know about the main focus of the plot doesn't mean you can't drop clues right and left. If the ultimate plot involves a reptile cult, perhaps the PCs find a snake-hilted wavy sword in a treasure cache, and they fight wave after wave of lizardfolk. In hindsight, they'll be perfect examples of "oh, those guys were totally reptile cult minions," but at the time they're just foes in a swamp. At the moment of discovery, the player characters figure out that all those bits of foreshadowing relate to a future clue.

Reversal

At the reversal, affairs go horribly wrong for the PCs because they lose in a critical way. They suffer the loss of momentum, resources, or friends. Accomplish this by using active villains: that is, rather than the monsters waiting for the PCs to approach them, the monsters seek out the PCs who have been snooping around their lairs, minions, or schemes, and either warn them off in no uncertain terms (possibly including a threat to an innocent third party) or attack them in force, thus preventing any future interference.

Everything goes from bad to worse in the reversal: key tools or magical items are removed. Allies abandon the cause. People lose hope, and the villagers all run for safer territory. The paladin's warhorse is fed poison oats and the wizard's familiar flees the scene.

Or you can use the "Hail Hydra" moment, when a previous ally betrays the heroes in devastating fashion. However, this option is a bit cliché when applied to the quest giver who hired the party in the first place. The best option is a minion, henchman, or even a companion animal or familiar suddenly showing a dark side and betraying the adventurers' plans and secrets to their enemies.

Change in View: Expanding Stakes

The change in view is the point in the plot when the situation goes from "ok, I think we've got this reptile cult handled" to "OMG, they're summoning Yarnoth-Char and we're not ready for that!" The change in view shows the players that the plot they thought they understood is more advanced, more dangerous, or more immediate than anticipated. Timelines are advanced, scope increases, and the stakes suddenly become much, much higher. The threat becomes global: the menace overshadowing one city is a threat to all humans, or the threat to the dwarven miners involves digging up an ancient earth demon with the backing of pure darkness and the horns of Ragnarok.

What form this takes can vary wildly, but in general the dungeon crawl changes from "hey let's find some treasure" to something more personal or compelling than mere loot. By more personal, I mean that the villain threatens a beloved mentor, or that villain is revealed to be a relative of a PC. A hero's immediate family sides with the bad guys or is duped into helping them. A member of the party is kidnapped (ideal when a player has to miss a session or two), or the powers or memories of a character are magically wiped out. This last one works especially well if some of the characters fail their saving throws to avoid the memory loss—and only one or two remember the great, world-shaking threat that the party has been working against.

By more compelling than loot, I mean a threat to the innocent or to the established order of the world. The leader of the paladin order is suddenly revealed as a scion of Hell. The threat of snake people attacking the city is revealed to have already undermined the city's castle and temple—which will soon collapse into giant sinkholes. Turn up the volume by preparing an escalation that reframes the cause that the PCs are fighting for.

THE END

Every great campaign benefits from a sense of fate, a little bit of perfect timing, a great reversal, and a twist that reveals more than anyone suspected at the start. You can improve your chances of delivering those thrills to your readers or players if you generate a conclusion and make all roads points to it. Indeed, this is the ideal way to structure foreshadowing, set clues, and otherwise drop hints to the ultimate end point: start with a sense of where the campaign will end, and evoking a sense of dawning realization by the players becomes easier. Don't be surprised if players guess correctly at your finale. All speculation, right or wrong, builds the suspense and anticipation toward "how it all turns out"—a moment, that, in an ideal campaign, you know of the gist of in advance.

TAKE A WALK ON THE DARK SIDE

Robert J. Schwalb

I could list many reasons why you shouldn't run a game featuring evil player characters, so many that banging out words to the contrary seems somewhat silly. After all, my own attempts to run evil campaigns have usually fallen apart after my players took the "evil" they had scribbled on their character sheets as a license to play psychopaths. Rather than seeing themselves as a team, they drew their knives and turned against one another in an orgy of violence; the quest, mission, and goal forgotten in the sheer chaos their antics created.

So, why bother?

COOL TOYS AND COOL CHARACTERS

Evil has the coolest toys. Sure, fantasy roleplaying games, especially those with *D&D* in their DNA, focus on creating and playing good or neutral characters accompanied by cute familiars and befriended by shining unicorns, but we're all drawn to the dark and sinister. Darth Vader remains a beloved character, even though he butchered a bunch of younglings and strangled his wife. Elric of Melniboné, Prince Jorg from the *Prince of Thorns*, Sand dan Glokta, Logen Ninefingers, and others from Joe Abercrombie's books, Glen Cook's *Black Company*, and many, many other sinister characters from books, film, and video games resonate with us, keep our attention, and fascinate us with their willingness to do whatever it takes. So while we might enjoy taking up the holy avenger and butchering some devils, sometimes we want to draw Stormbringer instead and gobble up some souls.

Ask anyone who's tried and they'll likely tell you that running adventures for evil characters is a bad idea. Player characters turn against each other. They wreak havoc on the setting. They murder, steal, and viciously assault everyone they meet. An evil character is the key to the locks we use to secure the chains we place on our ids. While I generally agree with this assessment, I do feel morally gray characters to be the most interesting characters since they're not above getting their hands dirty or doing questionable deeds to accomplish their goals. Such characters might be evil or they might be self-serving, but I think, with planning and preparation, you can create awesome and memorable stories with these sinister protagonists.

ACKNOWLEDGE THE RISKS

No matter how excited you are to experiment with a dark and gloomy game, it's not going to work without buy-in from your players. Tabletop roleplaying games (TRPGs) offer escape from the real world, letting people shed their lives and adopt different ones, even if only for a few hours. When we're inundated with real life news about murder, mayhem, war, and other atrocities, playing the parts of "evil's" agents might not be an attractive proposition. If you present the possibility to your players and a few would rather not descend into darkness, don't make a big deal about it. Do something else, or start a side group with the interested players.

Once everyone agrees to play in a dark game, you must take the time to have an open and frank discussion with the players to establish firm limits on the kinds of stories you will tell together. Do this not only for the players, but also for yourself. The game is supposed to be fun, and if it veers into uncomfortable territory, it stops being fun. Don't think you'll able to change how people react to certain topics in play; you won't. Not everyone will reveal their personal limits to the other players. They might feel weird about it, suspect others of using their limitations against them, or the topic could be particularly painful. For this reason, have an open discussion first and follow up with the players one-on-one to make sure everyone is fine with the game's darkness level. Once you establish these limits, keep them. Don't violate your players' trust by pushing against their comfort zones. If you force the issue, such games can break up even the tightest knit groups, souring and ruining friendships as a result.

ANTI-HEROES NEED TO STICK TOGETHER

Limitations on the sorts of subjects tackled in the game can keep dark groups functioning, but even the most restrained groups can fall apart if you're not prepared. Some players assume an evil nature frees their characters from the group dynamic, such that the characters can act with impunity against the other members, resorting to theft, betrayal, and even murder when the whim strikes them. Such characters become a cancer, eventually causing the team to unravel and the game to fall apart. In TRPGs, the stories the players tell involve an ensemble cast of characters, individuals who work better together than they do apart. Being evil (or not good) doesn't change this fact. The characters need each other if they want to achieve their goals and survive the adventures they undertake.

You can reinforce the group concept and encourage cooperation from even the most diabolical characters by inventing a group identity, something to which their characters can collectively belong. They might be members of a thieves' or assassin's guild, a debauched noble family, mercenary company, diabolical or esoteric cult, or other organization that engages in dark and sinister activities. While you can create the story wrapper yourself, you might find it has stronger appeal if you let the players decide instead during the first game session or pre-game discussion. Give the players time to create the identity, offering suggestions when necessary. When they settle on something, be sure to adapt the adventures you'd run to work within the stated identity to reinforce its importance and maintain its relevance at the table.

IRON FIST OF THE VILLAINOUS PATRON

The group construct suggests characters will be self-motivated, which affords them a bit more freedom to cause trouble. You can tighten the leash by giving the characters a patron, one much more powerful than the group and one with the means to crush them if they run amok. The PCs become henchmen. They undertake missions chosen by their patron to further his or her cause. The patron provides incentives for success and punishment for their failures. Eventually, the PCs might come to resent their patron and work to extricate themselves from his or her control. One or more PCs might even have designs on replacing the patron, which can provide a great ending to a long campaign, with the characters growing powerful enough to break their chains and take power for themselves.

If you use the patron route, you can create the character yourself, of course, but the patron might be stronger if you let the players decide. They might serve a lich, an evil dragon, a dark and brooding monarch, or even a demon lord. Once more, player investment in the story gives them ownership of it and a reason to see how the story unfolds.

COMMON ENEMIES AND PARALLEL MOTIVATIONS

As effective as fear of a patron can be in uniting a group, hatred of a common enemy might be even stronger. The source of hate might be a vengeful paladin the characters crossed at one point in the past. It could be an organization, such as a rival guild of thieves or the Inquisition. Then again, it could be a being of incredible power, a demigod with designs on advancing his or her status, a cunning necromancer who commands a nation of undead, or a tyrannical empress, with armies, assassins, wizards, and countless others firmly under her thumb. Directing the player characters' evil impulses outward helps keep them from turning against each other. However, to make this work, you need to supply a reason for each member of the party to despise the common enemy, preferably working the details into the characters' backgrounds or developing the animosity in the first adventure.

The methods you use to bind the group should suggest the underlying motivations for what the group does in the game. A band of cultists might seek glory in the name of their foul god, while mercenaries could chase wealth and infamy. Other groups might crave vengeance, going to great lengths to exact their wrath on the people who wronged them. Since evil groups tend to be more temperamental than those committed to virtue, it's best to tie their adventures, at least in tangential ways, to the motivating force. Doing so keeps them focused on their task and allows them to make at least some progress toward achieving their group's objective.

This said, evil characters do undertake many of the same kinds of adventures as good or neutral ones. Evil characters crave gold and gems, seek magical items, and hope to uncover knowledge to advance their personal aims and to increase power. The difference is in both in the reason and the methods.

WINNING WITH GREED AND SELFISHNESS

Dark characters tend to be self-serving. They do what they do because it benefits them. You wouldn't find an anti-paladin venturing into the dragon's lair to rescue the king's son who found himself caught in the monster's clutches. No, the anti-paladin would confront the dragon to steal its treasures, dismember the carcass for any valuable organs and scales, and then ransom the son to the king for a tidy profit. Similarly, a group of brigands might take on a group of orcs rampaging through the wilderness not out of the kindness of their hearts, but because the orcs are attracting attention to their own criminal enterprise, reducing the number of caravans passing through their lands. If not stopped, the orcs could dislodge the bandits from their favored haunts.

Thus, you can draw evil characters into the same adventures you would use for other characters provided you give them sufficient reason. Typically, you do this by giving the characters a stake in the story's outcome. When considering an adventure, take time to create hooks that specifically appeal to the characters' dark natures and their stated reasons for adventuring. For example, a published adventure might suggest the characters help a farmer by stopping thieves from stealing his prized hogs. A noble group might do so because it's the right thing to do. A more mercenary group might take the job for a reward. An evil group would likely hear about the valuable hogs and kill the farmer, only to have those hogs stolen by someone else. The party still becomes involved in the adventure, but they do so because the trouble affects them directly rather than someone they don't care about. Basically, most evil characters are me-first characters—their motivations are purely self-interested, and you can exploit this as a GM.

DARK DEEDS . . .

With the proper hook, evil characters can become involved in almost any adventure, but the methods they use to overcome the challenges can take the story in unexpected and dark directions. Evil characters don't think twice about using hirelings or slaves to venture down darkened corridors to spring all the traps. They might ally themselves with the enemies you hoped they would fight, perhaps even helping the adventure's villains accomplish their goals for the right price. Furthermore, they might abandon the adventure once they achieve their personal objectives, leaving the common folk to deal with the mess the party created. And if they complete the mission, there's probably nothing to stop the characters from taking everything and anything they want from the people they were ostensibly there to help.

While you might bristle at the horrors evil characters commit and their exploitation of innocents, this is what evil adventurers do. They aren't nice people; they do bad things, sometimes very bad things. Rather than steering them to take certain paths or to act against their natures, let the story unfold as it will. If the characters want to round up the villagers, sell them off as slaves, and burn down their houses, so be it. If they cut the throat of the princess they rescued from the ogre, let it happen. These and other atrocities are what evil characters do and that's the story you are helping to tell.

. . . LEAD TO BITTER TEARS

As important as it is to let the players portray their characters in a consistent manner, it is equally important to ensure their actions have consequences. Adventurers do not operate in a vacuum. The decisions they make can and should change the world around them. Evil characters who sack and burn temples eventually attract the attention of religious leaders, who then dispatch their forces to bring the party to justice. Murdering the king's daughter in her bedroom not only enrages the king, but also might destabilize the region because she was intended to wed the son of a rival nation and bring about a lasting peace. Her death ends the arrangement and the old tensions, and possibly war, resumes.

The actions of the evil characters can produce adventure hooks for good adventurers, assuming your world has such people. The longer the evil campaign runs, the more likely it becomes for a group of "heroes" to hunt for the evil PCs and attempt to take them out. This might become an ongoing issue or a series of encounters or adventures where the evil characters find themselves on the run from heroes or constantly find their dastardly plans thwarted by these do-gooders.

CHANGE OF PACE

Playing evil for its own sake can be fun, but such characters can feel boring after a time. There are only so many commoners to strangle, villages to burn, and demons to summon. Good player characters commonly face story hooks that test their virtue, putting them in difficult situations where they have to make hard choices. Evil characters usually choose the option that profits them the most. However, nothing says the characters have to remain evil. It might be interesting for evil PCs to find redemption, to leave behind the darkness in their hearts and do good deeds, even if they continue to employ dubious methods.

No matter how you go about it, whether you heed my advice or not, experimenting with evil characters can be a refreshing change of pace. It allows the players to see the world from the other side, to become the problem rather than its solution. No matter what preparations you make, however, evil groups rarely last. If they don't do themselves in, the forces of good and order eventually find them and, most likely, end them. And that's okay, right? In our heart of hearts, we want the good guys to win, even if the bad guys are more interesting characters.

OTHERWORLDLY VISIONS

Steve Winter

Tabletop RPGs command the great power to transport players to any setting or situation that can be imagined. There's no need to build sets or paint pictures. A good storyteller sends players' imaginations anywhere, from a deep cavern to the ocean floor to outer space to the land of dreams. Though many of these worlds are easily recognizable as simple variations on historical eras, common myths, and popular story genres, the most memorable ones depart sharply from our sense of everyday norms to veer strongly into otherworldly visions.

What do we mean by otherworldly? Literally, we're talking about scenes that seem to be of another world. Something that's unlike the world we know; dreamlike; surreal. Most of all, it's the unexpected, the contradictory, and the paradoxical. A scene or an encounter is otherworldly when it includes objects, creatures, and situations that don't quite belong, that don't fit the characters' or the players' expectations, and that lie outside players' experience of reality.

FROM THE USUAL TO THE UNUSUAL

A typical RPG outing follows a certain pattern: "Here's the situation, here's the mission, here's the monster, go deal with it." Everything is understood beforehand, at least in broad strokes. But invoking the unexpected is a key element in achieving an otherworldly atmosphere. The situation becomes otherworldly when characters run into something wholly outside their knowledge and experience. When they crash into an object or situation that can't be explained by science, magic, or religion, they've encountered something truly otherworldly. They'll need to stretch the boundaries of imagination to find an explanation, if they can find one at all.

H. P. Lovecraft, arguably the master of the otherworldly tale, outlined four ways otherworldliness can be conveyed in his 1937 essay titled "Notes on Writing Weird Fiction."

"There are, I think, four distinct types of weird story; one expressing a *mood or feeling*, another expressing a *pictorial conception*, a third expressing a *general situation, condition, legend*, or *intellectual conception*, and a fourth explaining a *definite tableau* or *specific dramatic situation or climax*."

In other words, he lays out four ways to express otherworldliness: through mood, through odd images or sensory inputs, through ideas or conditions that are troubling or surreal, and through actual situations or events that defy reality.

In an RPG, mood is the hardest of these to establish on its own. RPGs are different from fiction, in that mood seldom exists as a discrete, free-standing element. Mood arises organically in a roleplaying setting through the GM's skillful use of the other three elements: images, conditions, and events.

An alternative, but not quite as useful, way to categorize otherworldliness in RPGs is their scope. At the small end of the scale are very limited forays into the genre: one-off adventures that can be dropped into a mundane setting for a change of pace. Occupying the middle ground are settings that include otherworldly situations as exceptional phenomenon to be investigated or prevented: *Call of Cthulhu* is the prime example. At the top are entirely otherworldly settings: the seminal 1975 RPG *Empire of the Petal Throne* and 1985's *Skyrealms of Jorune* both drop characters into unique worlds where exploring the setting as a newcomer and learning its alien intricacies (and jargon) is a significant part of the fun.

TO BREAK THE RULES, FOLLOW THESE RULES

The first rule for a GM trying to create an otherworldly atmosphere is to resist over-explaining. GMs pour a lot of effort into creating settings, characters, and stories, so they love to give exposition in storytelling form. But otherworldly weirdness should be difficult, if not impossible, to comprehend. Explaining it is the last thing you want to do.

As GM, you can describe what characters see, hear, and smell, but don't interpret it for them. You're proud of your strange concoctions and want everyone else to appreciate them too, but once they're explained, they stop being amazing. Plants, animals, and buildings from an alternate reality might be so alien that they can't immediately be categorized as such. Describing something as "an alien plant" robs it of wonder. Describing it as "asymmetrically formed of yellow, paddlelike shapes sprouting multicolored cysts that seem to follow you as you move" not only leaves players wondering what in heck they're looking at (and what's looking at them), but also invites them to ask questions and actively investigate the scene.

The second rule is, don't overdo it. The weird shouldn't be commonplace. If everything is weird, then it all becomes mundane and nothing is weird. This rule has a corollary, however; sometimes it's OK to overdo it. The overdoing itself can be an anomaly, if things that should be rare suddenly become the norm and vice versa. Paradoxically, the rule still applies while you're breaking it: don't overdo the overdoing it.

The third rule is, steer away from standard monsters. "Monsters" are whatever foes the characters typically face, whether that's mythological creatures, space aliens, undead, kung fu gangsters, or owls and snakes that prey on feudal mice. No matter how strange the creatures in your game's monster collection might be, even if the characters have never encountered them before, the players are familiar with them. To create a sense of the weird, encountered creatures and NPCs must be outside the players' experience. This is one of the strengths of a post-apocalyptic game such as *Gamma World*: unique mutated monsters are so easy to create that every monstrosity the characters encounter can be something the players have never seen before.

Again there's a corollary, and this one can save the GM work; monsters that look familiar but act or fight in surprising ways perfectly suit the tone. For example, a warty, green-skinned troll that wears an embroidered vest, smokes with a cigarette holder, and speaks in a cultured New England accent probably isn't what the characters expect when they hear about a troll living under the bridge. The same goes for monsters that have a unique appearance but actually use standard, existing game statistics. For example, the yellow, paddlelike alien plant mentioned above could use the same game statistics as an off-the-shelf troll. This works as long as the deception isn't recognized by players.

This corollary can be expanded to trappings in general, whether you're looking at monsters, vehicles, weapons, magic spells, or anything else. If a sorcerer from the cadaverous realm of Qum needs a destructive spell, a simple fireball can be reskinned so that when it bursts, it momentarily forms the shape of a gigantic crystal skull, and everyone inside the skull takes 8d6 necrotic damage. The change in the damage type neatly reinforces the change in appearance. If you're doing things right, players will focus on the unfamiliar trappings and won't connect the dots to the familiar spell until later, if at all. *Empire of the Petal Throne* did this masterfully with its "eyes" (magical weapons) bearing names such as "the eye of joyful sitting amongst friends" (*charm person*) and "the eye of triumphant passage through infernos" (*immunity to fire*).

The fourth rule is, keep the game moving. If players have time to slow down and think about everything their characters are experiencing, scenes lose their impact. This is true in general, but it's doubly true when players confront scenes that are intentionally disorienting. Players need time to explore and appreciate the strangeness around their characters, but they can't be given enough time to figure things out. A sense of "this can't be right" is essential to maintaining otherworldliness.

HOW DO WE GET THERE?

By our definition, the otherworldly lies outside our experience of reality. No matter how good your imagination is, thinking up bizarre images and events wholly beyond your experience can be tough. To help, here are techniques to get things started.

Make It the Wrong Size. Small things become big, big things become small—or big things become stupendously big. Anything that's the wrong size gets our attention and triggers disturbing thoughts and questions, whether it's Jörmungandr, a snake so huge that it encircles the world, or a race of aliens so tiny they can build entire colonies in the quiet portions of our brains.

Combine and Divide. Take two or more creatures that don't belong together and make them one, or take one creature that seems indivisible and split it into two or more parts. The Greeks were masters of this, with their centaurs, harpies, medusae, and other mix-and-match monsters. The rearrangement doesn't need to be purely physical. Conflicting aspects of a being's personality might manifest as separate creatures, or as a creature and a statue, or as a rock and a weather effect. What appear to be conjoined twins could be loyalty and betrayal personified. *D&D's* xorn is an interesting example of this: part cross-dimensional horror, part gem-munching philosopher.

Betray the Senses. People become paranoid when they can't rely on the truth of what they see, hear, feel, or smell. Vision is the most obvious sense to play with because so many of our in-game descriptions involve what things look like. Objects or creatures that bend or alter light, or phase in and out of vision (or reality), or that look closer or farther away than they really are, or that appear to be one thing but are actually many things acting in concert, all make players question whether they can believe their senses. Putting the senses at odds with each other is another useful technique: a creature that's wreathed in ice, emanates heat, smells like the sea, and sounds like creaking timber when it moves should cause some perplexity. The adventure *The Monolith from Beyond Space and Time* offers a one-way journey into a realm where it's effectively impossible to look behind oneself, but that simple rule is so disorienting that characters who wander more than a few steps apart might never find each other again.

Ask "What If the Opposite Were True?" We navigate through life on a foundation of automatic assumptions: water flows downhill, fire is hot, night time is dark, fish can't read, plants don't complain, our thoughts are invisible to others. Consider what would happen if one of those too-obvious-to-question truths no longer held. What sort of society might characters encounter in a place where any particular rule had never been true? *White Plume Mountain's* stream flowing through air instead of across the ground leans in this direction.

Focus on Contradictions. We expect anything destructive to be loud and flashy: Consider movies where catapulted stones explode in flames when they hit the turf, and 200-lb. men shot with bullets weighing 8 grams are hurled 6 feet backward. Conversely, we expect a tiny silver bell to emit a pleasing tinkle. We're surprised if the bell unleashes a concussive wave that shatters windows, sets off car alarms, and hurls people backward (you know, like 8-gram bullets do in movies). Likewise, people expect a simple and predictable effect when they turn to the left. If something different happens—they're facing right, or straight up, or back the way they came from, or into the past—they're instantly disoriented. Playing with those types of contradictions can thoroughly disrupt players' expectations. In *Empire of the Petal Throne*, a horror of the underworld called the ssu smells like musty cinnamon, a jarring contrast of hideous monster and pleasant aroma.

Look to Other Mythologies. Since you're reading this essay in English, in an American publication, odds are you're from a Western culture and are chiefly familiar with European mythology. It's well worth your time to read mythology from other parts of the world. The themes tend to be the same no matter where the stories come from, but different cultures present those themes with very different trappings. As noted above, changing trappings can have huge effects on atmosphere, even if everything else remains the same. Hindu mythology is especially good in this regard if you're already steeped in Greek and Norse myths, but every culture has unique perspectives to offer. You can't go wrong by broadening your horizons.

You also can't go wrong by expanding your players' horizons with scenes, situations, and encounters that defy their expectations. The principles and techniques explained above should smooth your way into exploring unique, otherworldly realms for your games.

WHEN LAST WE LEFT OUR INTREPID HEROES

Embracing the episodic storytelling style—punchy, quick, and full of drama!—in your campaign

Clinton J. Boomer

What can we steal from television's tropes, idioms, and storytelling tools?

Anything that isn't nailed down, of course.

TAKING LIBERTIES WITH THE SOURCE MATERIAL

Real quick, before we begin, raise your hand if you love fantasy novels.

. . . you don't actually have to raise your hand, of course.

Not literally, anyway.

But my assumption—which I think is fair!—is that you're probably raising your hand right now, metaphorically at least.

After all: if you're the sort of GM who picked up this book to brush up on odd, clever little tricks and delve into the deepest unusual, mind-bending design insights, on the off chance that something found within such a tome might make your game the very best that it can be, well . . . you're probably also the sort of reader who loves great fantasy fiction in novel-length format.

Me too.

The thing is, though . . . not all of your *players* are necessarily going to be into slogging through all those hefty, classic literary fantasy texts, right?

Sure, most of your players have probably seen *The Hobbit* and *Lord of the Rings* . . . but have all of them *read* the whole series, too?

Maybe. Maybe not.

If one were so inclined, however, you could sit down—your entire player-group, all together—and watch a whole season of television as a crew.

It wouldn't even be hard.

Let's talk, then, about ways to tell "episodic stories" in your game: how to run adventures that combine all the things we love about great novels—the sweeping scope, the driving meta-plot, the epic setting—with all the quick, punchy, clever action, and crushing drama of really good, addictive television.

In a lot of ways, you see, can have the best of both worlds.

THE EPISODIC FORMAT

The episodic format assumes that each piece of the story builds on all of the parts around it, but that each "episode" tells a cohesive mini-tale with a satisfying beginning, middle, and end point . . . always leaving room for one more chapter.

So.

Do *you* use a short "Previously, On . . ." or a high-octane "highlight reel" or a swift "last game recap" at the very beginning of each game-session? Just to catch up super-quick on what happened recently, including the major plot elements and campaign-defining twists of your narrative?

I do, and I've found that a short, snappy, fast-paced game of "what awesome and interesting stuff do we all remember from the last few sessions?" can work absolute *wonders* for keeping the party—both in-character and out-of-character!—on track, immersed, and engaged with the campaign.

Sometimes, of course, scenes are recut: rearranged, re-edited, or recontextualized, with bits of heroism or villainy, cowardice or brutality, humor or drama slightly . . . *heightened*, perhaps. Exaggerated, amplified, and played up.

Sometimes, details change: a purely random encounter becomes a life-defining match of savage blades, bright woodland becomes darkest swamp, a thin drizzle becomes a cruel thunderstorm, gentle jibes become blood-vendetta, a short volley of dueling casters becomes an epic clash of earth-shaking spell-power.

Sometimes, we can be confronted with new perspectives: seeing an old scene though the fresh eyes of another witness, learning something scary or beautiful about how our own actions are seen from outside ourselves.

This? This is a *feature*, not a bug.

Honestly, I would no sooner quit doing those quick little pregame recaps than I would stop . . . I don't know, *using dice.*

Wait. No, I take that back. I would *totally* stop using dice first, actually. Diceless systems can be awesome!

The point is that "last game recaps" are an element—stolen, whole cloth!—right out of serialized, episodic fiction . . . and they happen to work *exceptionally* well within the context of a weekly or biweekly campaign.

Even if they *aren't* a part of novel-length fantasy.

In fact, a lot of things that might aid your campaign can be lifted straight out of television's tropes, idioms, and storytelling tools. Your game, like episodic television, has a lot of inborn advantages that a novel simply doesn't have . . . and you can exploit those advantages for fun and profit!

PLAYER-DRIVEN, CHARACTER-FOCUSED

A novel, good or bad, is finished before you start it: from the moment you pick up a book, the ending is set in stone. There's nothing you can do or say while reading Chapter 1 that will influence what happens on the final page.

But a serialized story—whether on television, produced as comics, or shot on film—has a little more . . . *flexibility.*

The showrunners might bring back a particular fan-favorite villain or kill off a much-beloved side-character, a running joke might be developed into something much bigger, friendships might blossom into romance just as romance might sour into hatred, or the whole thing might take a bizarre left turn at the season finale only to set everyone up for something amazing later down the line.

The writers and producers are listening: watching, reading, and analyzing what fans and critics alike are saying.

And they react accordingly.

A good game should feel the same way: naturalistic, semi-improvisational, and unscripted, all set against a depth of field that suggests that you—the director, the writer, the GM!—know exactly what's going on behind every rock and tree, with rules and stats and secrets prepared for every eventuality.

PCs in a game, likewise, are more similar to the characters in our favorite TV shows than those within static texts. Actors age, they leave the cast to pursue other projects, they have kids, they get injured on-set, they adopt new wardrobes or want to bring new twists and challenges to a stale role.

Similarly, players mature and grow just as their characters reach higher and higher levels: if you look at the difference between a 3rd-level PC and the same character at 17th level, it's not a difference of "beginning of the novel to end of the novel" . . . it's a difference of "Season 1 to Season 8."

The great thing about your game is that you can let your PCs grow into new roles, always knowing that the arc of your campaign is as long as it needs to be!

TITLE: SERIES & EPISODE (AND THE EPISODE GUIDE!)

So . . . what's the *name* of your game?

Do your players have it written down?

On their sheets?

Oh, sure: your players most likely know the name of the system, and they even probably know the name of your setting; if you're playing through a published Adventure Path or a mega-dungeon or a classic boxed set, your players most likely know which one it is from the initial setup.

But my guess is that your players probably *also* have a pet nickname for your game, whether it's "Tuesday Night *D&D*" or "Jen's game at the coffee shop" or "that slugfest in Mike's basement with all the damn orcs."

You can control this.

You can *take command* of it.

Give your campaign an official name, as if it were a licensed and published book or Adventure Path of its very own. Refer to your game by its *name*, the same way people talk about *Game of Thrones* or *Arrow* or *Sherlock* or *Buffy* or *Supernatural* or *The Walking Dead* . . . and your players will follow suit.

After all: the Marvel cinematic universe has a lot going on. We don't expect the same things from *Guardians of the Galaxy: Volume 2* that we'll expect from Season 3 of *Jessica Jones*—and with good reason! —despite the fact that both series take place in a single shared continuity . . . and the title gives us the first hint as to what we should expect.

Once you have a title for your game, the next step is generating a quick and punchy title for each session. You don't have to name each "episode" before it "airs," of course, but having an idea what you *would* call the session that's about to be run can give you surprising insight.

After a session, decide on the official name for the night's activities. This doesn't have to be a clever play on words, necessarily—or an extended metaphor or a reference to the recurring themes and literary devices in your game—it just has to encapsulate what differentiates *this* session from the episodes around it.

If the PCs encounter goblins carousing during one of their seasonal celebrations, for example, you can call the session "Goblin Fest!"

Then, when you do a recap, you can refer back easily: instead of saying "three games ago," you can say "During the events of *Goblin Fest 2016*. . . ."

This is useful in all sorts of unexpected ways. Give it a try, and you might be delighted with the results as the references become more and more natural.

OPENING MUSIC; ICONIC SOUNDTRACK

So, what comes after every good recap on TV?

The opening theme music and the credits, of course!

As an aside: do you—as a GM—use Action Points?

Or . . . I don't know, Drama Points?

Luck Points, Hero Points, or something else vaguely similar?

I'm not going to say that you *should* use them, since that could be the topic of another—longer and more complicated!—essay. Instead, I'll suggest that you reward a player (or players) for acting as your official sound mixer, and that Plot Points or the like make a fine, cheap reward system.

And yes, you need a hard-working sound mixer: not just a DJ, playing a few recurring songs or snippets of familiar background music here and there, but an active participant. Someone making sure that the auditory landscape surrounding you illuminates what's on the table.

If it works for TV, steal it!

And you've got an advantage that TV shows don't have: you don't need to care about copyright.

If you want to open each session with "Stairway to Heaven," play "One Winged Angel" from *Final Fantasy VII* during each climactic fight with that one iconic boss, and then end each session with Moby's "God Moving Over the Face of the Waters," you can *totally do that*.

Just be sure to throw a few Director's Points toward your sound engineer!

MAKING YOUR CAMPAIGN LIVELY

Joss Whedon is your master now.

When you embrace the episodic style, you declare there will be no such thing as a "forgettable" episode, even if it's a breather. What does that mean?

Punchy: Most characters are, at the end of the day, murder-hobo monster hunters propelled by bloodlust, fear, and greed. *This is okay.* Throw them a series of good hooks, bad hooks, memorable baddies, one-shot villains, and season-long arcs—spiced with a mix of mysteries, heists, dungeon crawls, and courtly intrigue—then let *them* pick what's most appealing.

Quick: Don't dwell on anything that isn't interesting. If an in-character task in your game is getting bogged down, look up the relevant rules *once*; if the rules aren't thereafter being applied at least once every other episode, feel free to handwave them from that point forward. And never, ever be afraid to fast-forward six months of in-game time!

Full of Drama: Let your players feel for their characters, even if—especially if!—those feelings are bad. This game is about betrayal and hatred, glory and terror, righteous anger and furious vengeance. Don't skimp on letting the PCs sit quietly in the rain, every once in a while, staring down the side of the cold mountain and shaking with rage while their old lives burn.

WRAPPING IT ALL UP

In conclusion: Sure, we all love *Lord of the Rings*.

We adore *Harry Potter*, too, along with *His Dark Materials* and the *Dark Elf Trilogy*. We thrill and swoon to *A Song of Ice and Fire* and *The Dark Tower*; we hang upon *The Name of the Wind* and *The Wise Man's Fear*; our lives and our games are enriched by devouring the *Bas-Lag* books and the *Gentleman Bastard Sequence*.

Our shared passion of *gaming* springs from a love of fantasy novels, and I'll freely admit that I haven't read enough of them.

I *have*, however, seen enough television—good, bad, and also-ran—to last ten or more lifetimes.

And it's likely that at least some of your players are in the same boat.

Therefore, remember this if nothing else. The more you can steal from the medium of television, the more your players will treat your game like an event: something to look forward to, week after week, tuning in again and again.

Tricks from the Oral Tradition

Kevin Kulp

Roleplaying games are shared constructed stories: the GM and the players work together to build a cohesive narrative, layering elements together to form an ongoing tale. Just as a story can change with every telling, using varying methods when presenting an adventure can inspire new possibilities from standard templates. We'll discuss techniques from traditional storytelling that can help make RPGs amazing, both in terms of pacing and presentation.

THE POWER OF STORY

If you picture an adventure like music, it wouldn't be a low flat hum, identical in tone and pitch throughout the duration of the song. Instead, it'd be more like a great symphony: periods of great power and thunder (combat), quiet sections of slower music (mystery investigation or roleplaying encounters), repeating themes that interweave throughout the piece, and building tension that resolves itself in a climactic movement. After each game, ask yourself how the music from that game would sound. If it's not what you'd like, make changes for the next game.

Pacing the Adventure

The best adventures have an ebb and flow to them, an adrenaline-filled series of events followed by a chance for players to regroup, catch their breath, and try a different type of encounter (whether roleplaying, combat or investigation). If you ever hear of an adventure that players say is a "grind," it likely refers to poor pacing and repetition in the challenge and encounter structure. Even the most interesting combats bog down when there are too many fights in a row.

To help prevent this, take a lesson from the pacing of storytelling and provide a variety of different scenes or challenges. Just as in the real world, there are many problems in a fictional game world that violence (or the threat of violence) can't solve. Challenges can be political struggles, mystery investigations linked together by strings of clues, fiendishly clever traps, or traditional combat encounters. If you tie these together (a fight in a trapped room, or roleplaying with powerful guild leaders as you try to identify a murderer) you'll help prevent your game from feeling stale.

Similarly, vary the stakes for winning or losing a confrontation. In some fights, the stakes may simply be that the heroes die or are defeated. In political encounters, the entire future of empires might be decided because the heroes made a pretender to the throne look bad in public. If you vary the stakes, you'll keep your players intrigued. Ask yourself "what's the worst possible consequence?" and see if it's interesting enough to include.

Improvisation

Many people find the best adventures happen when they don't over-prepare. That's a hard leap of faith for some GMs, but the trick is trusting your knowledge of the game and your world to allow improvisation on the fly.

The best way to prove this to yourself is to hold an occasional game where you do absolutely no preparation at all. At the start of the game, ask each player what their hero's current goal is. Then build the game session on the fly to help at least one hero move closer to their goal. You'll have to pull monsters out of the book, but you'll learn more about pacing for your personal group than you would from a published adventure.

Plot and Presentation

Professional storytellers learn the hard way that exposition sucks away momentum and can stop a story dead in its tracks. Find a different way to communicate that same information, however, and the audience stays riveted. The same is true for RPGs. Do your best not to narrate a string of facts; instead, help the players learn the same information through the environment, through NPCs, or through action.

Story through environment: Video games are great at communicating story through environment. Random graffiti, short diaries and logs, signs of struggles, lighting and architecture; all these elements can communicate history and events more effectively than exposition. In a dungeon, for instance, a corpse near a tapped wine barrel shows the heroes that the wine is deadly. Paintings of a princess with the princess's eyes gouged out from each painting communicates that someone—maybe the princess herself?—

hates her appearance. Dungeon architecture consisting of inaccessible, winding tunnels suggests a monster that can both fly and burrow (or disintegrate) is nearby, foreshadowing a deadly combat encounter.

Always think about how your adventure's physical environment might foreshadow and reinforce campaign events, NPC personality, and upcoming combat.

Story through NPCs: Exposition becomes a lot more interesting and a little less painful when the heroes can tease it out of a NPC during a conversation. This lets you answer natural questions from the players instead of reading them a list of facts. You can also combine both methods, starting with a NPC conversation and summing up known facts at the end to save time.

NPCs communicate facts from their own viewpoint, and those facts might be highly biased; you can take advantage of an unreliable narrator, feeding the players false information from someone who doesn't know or want to admit the truth.

Story through action: Describing action scenes can give your players just as much information as exposition. Instead of saying a castle is structurally unstable, for instance, you describe goblins shuffling carefully across an old bridge toward the heroes instead of running full tilt into battle. Instead of saying that there's a boss monster that the goblins don't want to awaken, you describe the goblins shushing one another and fighting in silence, biting back screams when they get hurt. How and where adversaries fight can reinforce themes or foreshadow future conflicts.

Marking the turning points: Any well-designed adventure has one or more points when the plot or the action can take dramatically different routes. This might happen when speaking to important NPCs, at the climactic end to an adventure, or when the players decide what tactics and strategy they're using for their next adventure. Most sections of an adventure feature steady and predictable action, but a pivot point can completely change the course of a campaign.

- Do the heroes adopt the pathetic but lovable kobold spy, or kill him?
- Do the heroes kill the kidnapped king because he's insulting and superior, or do they return him to the throne?
- Do the heroes destroy the ancient evil artifact, or draw on its power?

Anticipate these possibilities when you design your adventures, and milk them for everything they're worth. Present your players with difficult decisions. Let your players' decisions change the game world, for better or for worse. These difficult and far-reaching choices improve the game world and the campaign experience. For instance, if the heroes are asked to politically support either a friendly but incompetent ruler or a hostile but incredibly competent pretender to the throne, their decisions will become the tipping point for the future of the campaign.

THE POWER OF VOICE

As a GM, your voice is an essential tool. You can use it to awe your players, to create widely varied NPCs who sound nothing alike, and to hint to players when they should exercise caution or forge ahead. If you're always having NPCs speak in the third person by telling your players "He says . . .", you might be selling yourself and your game short.

No actors required: Don't ever feel like you need a background in acting to roleplay a hero or a NPC. Far from it. Your goal is to make an interesting character come alive, and there are ways to do that without leaping out of your comfort zone. If your players remember anything about the character after the fact, if the character doesn't blend into the background of the campaign's history, then you did your job.

Lean on stereotypes: Start by taking advantage of gaming stereotypes. Northern barbarians (both male and female) are powerful, blunt and gruff. Rogues are city-born, sly, and untrustworthy. Dwarves have deep voices and compare things to rocks. Elves are light-hearted and distrust civilization.

Do not, however, sink to offensive stereotypes, especially in regard to real-world nationalities or ethnicities. That's not going to make anyone's game more fun.

Starting with a stereotype (especially when you don't have a specific handle on how to roleplay a character) gives you common ground with your players, and it acts as shorthand for who they're speaking with. If you describe the old man in the tavern wielding a long staff, wearing a big floppy hat, and stroking a long white beard, they will immediately assume "wizard" without you ever having to say the word.

Break stereotypes: People don't particularly remember stereotypical characters after the fact; they do remember the characters who turned those stereotypes on their heads. When you want someone memorable, challenge expectations. Whether it's a pathetic urchin girl who's secretly an overlord of crime, a kobold with an amazing speaking voice, or a claustrophobic dwarf, surprising your players is a tremendous amount of fun that helps stretch the boundaries of your world.

Speech patterns: Some characters talk quickly. Some pause at awkward times. Some use huge words when a simple word would do, or prefer to speak in florid overwrought prose with far more words than they need (Alexandre Dumas, I'm looking at you). Speech patterns are simple for any GM to experiment with, don't require you to talk in anything other than your normal speaking voice, and provide a huge amount of context and information about what a NPC is like.

Accents (or "don't do them"): A lot of GMs think that roleplaying a NPC means using an accent. We recommend you give it a pass, or use accents only sparingly. Here's why: it's really hard to do a real-world accent properly, and messing it up will immediately drag your players out of their suspension of disbelief. Most GMs are better off using speech patterns and tonality to distinguish their characters, or even creating a fantasy accent, instead of trying to adapt a real-world accent to the cause.

Volume: How loudly or softly you speak when roleplaying a NPC can have a huge effect on how much your players pay attention. Quiet NPCs are either shy or believe what they are saying is so important that everyone around them should quiet down to listen; usually, that's exactly what happens. Loud NPCs are usually frantic, upset, or bombastic. A character who varies between loud and soft speech to emphasize points is someone who understands how to manipulate crowds, and how to use silence to make a point.

Speaking of which, silence is an incredibly powerful tool in public speaking, and that holds true for gaming as well. Knowing when to be briefly silent and let your players hang on your next word is a great technique for keeping people focused.

Clarity: How clearly you speak indicates how forcefully you want the NPC to come across. Mumble, and no one will listen or take your character seriously. Enunciate and speak with clarity, and they'll assume that the character believes what they're saying.

Tonality: What's the different between a shifty, lying informant and a proud, misinformed holy warrior? Tonality, at least in part. It doesn't involve an accent, but how you pitch your voice really carries the personality of the character. A child might be higher pitched, a giant might be low pitched, and a confused old man could be querulous. The more forceful a character, the stronger and more authoritative they're perceived; the more timid or frail a character, the weaker they're perceived. Similarly, whether someone is funny and has a sense of humor, or is dour and can't understand jokes, all falls under tone as well.

Body language: It's not just your voice that carries the character. Your body language does as well. Consciously change your body language for each NPC you play. You can sit up straighter, or hunch your shoulders, or purposefully fidget with nervousness as you speak. More honest and forthright characters have better posture, stubborn characters will cross their arms and legs, insane characters might twitch or cringe (for the type of insanity you see in fantasy gaming, at least), and lying characters avoid other peoples' gazes and will frequently touch their own faces.

Mannerisms go hand in hand with body language. Your players might not remember Karel the Dockmaster by name, but they'll remember the untrustworthy man with greasy black hair who liked to cough into his hand and then run his fingers through his hair. Trust me on this.

Giving your players hints: You can use your voice to subtly encourage your players to exercise restraint if their heroism is about to get them all killed, or to forge ahead when you're bored because they're spending all their time listening at closed doors. An occasional "Are you sure?" or "Really?", asked in a questioning tone, gives observant players a chance to reconsider a rash action. A clear and breezy "nope, you check and there's no sign that anyone here ever learned to set traps" gives them the encouragement needed to move more quickly in their investigations. Play with this meta-knowledge to help steer the group; if you describe one corridor in a darker, more foreboding tone than a different corridor, you'll help communicate the danger and fear facing the heroes to their players as well.

Once your players are familiar with this technique and expect it, you can sneakily turn it around on them. For instance, imagine a party of heroes facing a powerful group of telepaths. As GM, you might tell them in a straightforward manner, "nope, attacking them would be a terrible idea. You're sure of it. You should reconsider it." In this case, you're not giving the players direct advice, even though your voice sounds like it; instead, you're roleplaying the telepaths surreptitiously influencing the heroes' decision-making process, and you're doing it by messing with the players instead of their characters. You don't want to pull this trick very often, but when you do, it's both fun and memorable for players who put it together.

Distinctive NPCs are made, not born. Find a hook—whether voice, mannerisms, tone, or personality—and hang the rest of their character on it. Remember, not every NPC needs all these techniques, and it's perfectly fine to signify the less important bit players in your world by the fact that they all sound exactly the same. Doing so might even make your more developed and important NPCs stand out more quickly.

PUTTING IT ALL TOGETHER

Don't be shy about trying one or two of these techniques per game. After all, you'll never make the game even more fun unless you take some risks, and there's never a better place to take risks than among friends.

Action Scenes: More Than Just Flashing Blades

Margaret Weis

Action sequences are fun to write, fun for the reader to read, and fun for gamers to play. Action scenes should serve a purpose, however, or they look as though they have been tossed into the novel or game session to liven up an otherwise dull tale. In an RPG campaign, players become more involved in an action scene if they know they strive for a greater goal and are not just fighting bugbears because the Gamemaster needed something to fill the dungeon chamber.

Depending on the outcome the writer or GM wants to achieve, action scenes can be light-hearted or tense and dramatic. Light-hearted action scenes can be useful toward the beginning and middle of a story to engage interest and provide a laugh, even if that laughter is nervous laughter. Please note that such scenes simply don't work for some novels or game scenarios. If the GM is running a serious campaign and the players are deeply committed to the quest, the action scenes should reflect the nature of the game. Same with an author writing a novel about a serious subject—sometimes there's no place for humor.

Action sequences that appear near the end of a story are likely to be dramatic. The main characters are in danger. They are fighting for their lives as they struggle to achieve their goals. The readers or players know these characters, fear for them, want them to succeed, and hang on every word and deed. Unless the writer is a humorist writing a funny novel, a light-hearted action scene at this point can strike a jarring note.

When developing action scenes or thinking about where you want to place them in an RPG campaign, consider the setting and the purpose you need these scenes to serve.

ACTION SCENES THAT INTRODUCE CHARACTERS

Sometimes aspiring writers start their novels with rousing action scenes because they think this will capture the reader's interest. But if the readers haven't been given time to learn about the characters, they won't care whether the characters live or die.

When I was an editor at TSR, I read a novel proposal that started with a fight between a knight and the dragon. The knight was meant to be the hero, but the dragon had all the best lines and was by far the more interesting character. At the end of the fight, I was extremely disappointed when the knight killed the dragon. If the writer had allowed me to know the knight before hurling him into a battle with a dragon, I might have felt differently. As it was, that action scene did not work.

Light-hearted action sequences at the start of a novel can both engage the reader and serve to introduce the characters. In the novel *The Three Musketeers*, Alexander Dumas uses an extended action sequence that is both exciting and light-hearted to enliven the beginning of the book and, most important, to introduce the reader to the main characters.

This excellent example is found in chapter four, titled: "The Shoulder of Athos, the Baldric of Porthos and the Handkerchief of Aramis." Our hero, d'Artagnan, is in pursuit of his mortal enemy. While chasing after the villain, he manages to accidentally barge into the wounded Athos, become entangled in Porthos's cloak, and inadvertently places Aramis is a comprising position with a lady. All three of the aggrieved musketeers demand satisfaction for the insults and our hero is forced to defend his honor in the famous duel that results in the four becoming fast friends.

In this scene, Dumas not only provides exciting action, he uses that action to give the reader insight into each of his characters. In scenes that follow, we care about what happens to them.

The same type of action sequence can be useful in an RPG session at the start of a new campaign. By using an action scene to introduce players to their characters, to each other, and to the rules of the game, the GM conveys important information through action instead of through dialogue. Since the action takes place at the start of the game, it should be exciting and fun, not deadly. After all, you don't want the campaign to end before it even begins.

Even the clichéd scenario of heroes meeting in a tavern can work if the GM adds action and conflict. The player characters might be strangers to each other at the start of the game, but if they are Browncoats in an Alliance bar on Unification Day, they are going to become extremely good friends in a hurry.

Action scenes also present excellent opportunities to introduce critical NPCs, useful allies, and even continuing villains. The characters don't just hear about a dastardly plot to poison the town well; they interrupt the perpetrator in the middle of the act, but the scoundrel vanishes before he can be captured or killed. The next time the PCs encounter the villain, they know each others' faces and already have reason for immediate enmity.

ACTION SCENES THAT RELIEVE TENSION

The introduction of humor into a tense action scene can both relieve the tension and at the same time heighten it. The classic scene where Indiana Jones is confronted by the saber-wielding villain in the middle of a chase is a good example. We expect the usual epic swashbuckling duel and are not prepared for the logical response, which is the hero simply drawing his pistol and shooting the guy. The scene gives us a break in the tension by evoking laughter. In addition, it serves a purpose by providing insight into Indy's world-weary character.

In an RPG setting, an NPC can serve this role. The befuddled NPC wizard tries to help the heroes escape the prison wagon. Unfortunately, she does so by casting a *fireball* spell that sets the wagon on fire. The players escape, though with a few singed eyebrows.

The players can also bring a touch of humor to the game, as long as the actions they take are appropriate to their characters and to the situation. Jayne might decide to wear the hat his mama knit him while trying to rescue Mal from Niska's torture chamber. A resourceful GM could find all sorts of ways to bring Jayne's signature hat into the action.

ACTION SCENES THAT ADVANCE THE PLOT

An action sequence can be used to accomplish multiple tasks. This scene from *Storm Riders*, the second novel in my *Dragon Brigade* series, not only provides a break from previous scenes featuring court intrigue and lots of talking, it also advances the plot.

At this point in the novel, my co-author Robert Krammes and I needed to place our heroes in danger, force them to take action, and also reveal that they are in a world of trouble. We also needed for them to survive what could potentially turn into a lethal encounter.

The hero Stephano and his friend Rodrigo arrive home in the middle of the night to find assassins waiting for them. Stephano and one assassin are fighting in the bedroom when they hear police whistles. The assassin takes a header out the window, leaving Stephano to wonder how the police knew he and Rodrigo were under attack. At last he realizes they couldn't possibly have known. They are here for another reason.

"Let him go!" Stephano yelled to his friend. "The police aren't coming for him. They're coming for you!"

Thus we not only plunge the heroes into exciting action, we let them discover that they have multiple enemies and that it might be a good idea for them to leave town for awhile. We also let them live to fight another day, but we do so while further complicating their lives.

In an RPG campaign, the GM can use a situation like this to spring something completely unexpected on the players. In this instance, not only do the player characters have to fight off assassins, they have to decide what to do when they find out the authorities are after them.

During a game, it can be easy to lose sight of the reasons behind an action scene in the excitement of the moment, especially during combat. Remember that good action scenes not only provide action, they move the story forward. An action scene should be the culmination of the scene or scenes that came before it, while also motivating characters and setting up scenes to come. Good scenes show us what's happening, they don't tell us about it. An action scene should contain a definite emotion or mood, whether it's light-hearted, scary, full of tension, or ripe with hatred—the heroes', the villains', or both. Characters should have clear motivations so that the NPCs aren't just hostile bystanders waiting for the PCs to show up so they can do their thing.

An action scene should advance the plotline of the story. Actions taken by the characters can send ripples throughout the story line. When writing an action scene, give thought to how the scene might affect characters not directly involved and how the actions they take could later come back to bite the characters. This works especially well in an RPG setting. For example, the player character, Aramis, fights a duel with one of the cardinal's guards, who flees the scene. The king hears of the fight and gloats over the cardinal's defeat. Angry, the cardinal decides to prove that Aramis is having an affair with the queen and has his agent steal a necklace Aramis has given the queen. Her Majesty discovers the loss and pleads with Aramis and his friends to save her honor by recovering the necklace before the cardinal can give it to the king. The player characters now find themselves in a dangerous situation they could not have anticipated.

ACTION SCENES THAT POSE A CHALLENGE

Action doesn't necessarily mean combat. Or, at least, it doesn't have to mean only combat. The best action scenes in RPG sessions pose a challenge that the PCs must overcome in an active and (hopefully) exciting way. In a game session, action can be a chase, a puzzle with a time limit and deadly consequences, navigating a trapped-filled chamber, escaping from a collapsing ruin, or figuring out how to stop a ritual before the portal opens and the demon appears. Each and every one of these scenes can be designed to have all kinds of action that the PCs must accomplish to succeed, but you can also introduce an enemy to up the stakes and make the scene even more action-packed. It all depends on the needs of the adventure's story and the goals of the player characters.

WHY IS THIS HAPPENING?

Every action scene needs to have a reason for existence. Both the protagonists and the antagonists should be motivated to take action, and the action they take needs to be logical or the reader (or the players) won't believe in it.

In the example from Dumas, d'Artagnan has a strong motive for rushing down the stairs in pursuit of his nemesis. Athos, Porthos, and Aramis are strongly motivated to challenge d'Artagnan to a duel because he has bumped into one of them and accidentally discovered the secrets of the other two.

In *Storm Riders*, Stephano hears police whistles and knows that the constables are coming for Rodrigo. He has to let the assassin escape to save himself and his friend from being taken to prison. Conversely, when the assassin hears the police whistles, he knows he needs to save himself and he can't stick around to finish off our heroes.

In RPG campaigns, it's just as important for both the player characters and the nonplayer characters to be motivated to take action. This could be as simple as the PCs setting out to steal the dragon's treasure, or they could have a noble and lofty goal, such as fighting dragons to save the world from the Queen of Darkness. The dragon could be attacking the player characters simply because she's hungry, or she could be doing something vital for the war effort by protecting the sacred Disks of Mishakal.

Give thought to your action scenes before you write them. Don't just toss in a bar fight for the sake of having a bar fight. Make that fight work for you. Actions have consequences, as the saying goes, and that is certainly true than when writing novels and designing RPG adventures. Just remember that unlike a novel, when you design an RPG adventure your goal isn't to determine what the player characters do. That's up to the players! The GM's job is to set up exciting situations with many possible outcomes and then make adjustments on the fly as the players interact with those situations. Every action the players take alters the situation and advances the story—usually in ways you never expected! That's the fun of roleplaying games.

Just keep that in mind when you're wearing a brown coat into an Alliance bar on Unification Day. Anything can happen, and it will probably be exciting—one way or another!

TONE AND BOMBAST

Wolfgang Baur

O ther chapters of this volume talk about the mechanics and techniques of your story. This one is about how you choose to tell it. For high fantasy storytelling, I fear that all too often, our own homebrewed stories, the ones nearest and dearest to our hearts, are stunted by caution and cowardice. I speak from some experience on this.

BAROQUE STYLE VS. REALISTIC FANTASY

When I was starting out as a Dungeon Master, I wanted nothing as much as true heroes and a realistic story. I hated phony everything: phony swords as big as a ladder, bogus spiky armor and bare midriffs, moustache-twirling villains. I wanted fireballs, sure, but *credible* fireballs. I wanted cliffs and mountains, but not random 5,000 foot cliffs and mountains into the vacuum of space. There should be a reasonable economy. Lairs shouldn't feature random lava. Villains didn't need to sound like Russian mobsters or goose-stepping Nazis. I wanted subtlety in my fantasy, and I encouraged realistic characters, even though it was clear that some of my players were looking for a wahoo world of chaos magic, half-slaadi villains, and hissing drow priestesses ready to kill the paladin's dog.

I've since changed my mind about most of this. There's nothing wrong with gritty, small, grind-it-out campaigns full of verisimilitude and remarkable realism. They can be delightful, especially for genres like noir or modern mercenaries or even historical drama. But for the biggest impact—and the best results from your players—I urge you to be brave and embrace the largest, wildest themes of your campaign.

CAUTION IS THE ENEMY

Here's the thing about caution. When you spend a lot of prep time on matters of encumbrance, climate, and carefully thought-out schemes, you are not spending time on the elements of the game that players react to most strongly. The greatest moments of every one of my campaigns or adventures have been the ones where someone does something remarkably foolish, brave, self-sacrificing, or just plain dumb. And while we think of this as the purview of players, I'd argue that they take their cues from you, the Gamemaster who sets the tone.

For example, consider a goblin tribe that has found a way to summon one of the Great Walkers of the Wastes, a void entity of incredible power that will allow them to—finally!—breach the walls of a human city and conquer their foes of the last 50 generations. Standard plot, perhaps. But it could be designed in many ways. And I'd suggest that having the sniveling, cowardly goblins suddenly show remarkable, even suicidal bravery will make a huge impression on the players. Rather than a standard goblin fight, design the first encounter with this tribe as one where the goblins fight for what they see as impossibly high stakes.

If the goblins give their all, that means not only do the warriors fight to the last, but so do the goblin women and children. Goblin elders trip the adventurers, and the wounded never retreat. They make a last stand, and perhaps only the shaman escapes. The PCs wind up wiping out the village. The goblins defend a particular portal ferociously, and they pass along a scroll case from hand to hand, like an Olympic torch. When the scroll passes through the portal to the escaping shaman, the portal closes, and the remaining goblins commit suicide or just give up. Their goal is won.

I'm betting the players will be more interested in this than in the usual goblin encounter. That's the power of going overboard with your story style.

BIBLICAL BEATS, FANTASTIC FLOURISHES

Easy to say, perhaps, but how do you implement tone and theme in your story? In a nutshell, the main element in a baroque, high-powered narrative is a series of huge stakes and broadly constructed foes.

Think of the various books of the Bible: the ones full of "who begat whom" and various dietary laws are, frankly, the boring ones. The most interesting stories are the ones with big changes: creation and death, entire cities reduced to salt, floods, genocide, violence, and murder. Big, bold stories require that horrible things happen to your fictional world, so figure out which assassinations, mass murders, enslavements of entire cities, or abductions of the wise and the good are essential to your plots. In each case, apply what I call the Pulp Fiction rule: Is there any way to make the threat more intense? Can the villains taunt the heroes? Can an innocent bystander illustrate the cruelty of the opposition? Can the magic be more widespread, affecting hundreds instead of dozens, or spreading plague in hours instead of weeks? Take your reasonable story point and do at least one of the following three things to it:

- Make it personal or visceral
- Make it unfair
- Make the headline worse

We'll look at each technique in turn.

PERSONAL AND VISCERAL

Player characters are genuinely heroic badasses. They take a lot of damage and keep coming; they command magic and mighty weapons. So you sometimes need to hit them in unexpected ways: dropping a magic-dampening zone down on them would certainly be one way to do it. Specifically personal attacks are more effective, though. Drag in family and friends (if you can), and threaten the characters' wellsprings of power and authority. The aftermath of an earthquake provokes general horror; revealing that one of the earthquake victims is a beloved cousin incites personal outrage.

Likewise, personal story beats can attack or at least undermine a character's reputation—villains are certainly not above smear tactics. So if a necromancer's scroll includes the name of a paladin's ancestor, that's going to get a unwelcome bit of attention from a church inquisitor. A druid whose name is invoked by fire elementals as "the master of the great Pyroclasm of the Greenwood" might be mistrusted by the Captain of Rangers.

Sometimes, all it takes is the right level of description: the most common cheats are using children in danger (overdone but effective), or threatening a character's power directly (heavy on mechanics).

Describing a vat of blood or a pit of slime with sensory cues is always good practice, but to make the scene truly baroque, add hints of where the goo came from. A dog's skull and a half-slimed pair of shoes makes it clear that the slime has an origin. Sensory cues make a place or an encounter rise above the ordinary; the more important an encounter is, the more little moments of disgust, wonder, or fear you want to prepare ahead of time. Cues can be as simple as mentioning the number of dead crows under a particular tree, so it's always worth setting the scene with details specific to the mood you want to evoke.

"UNFAIRNESS"

Nothing is more unfair than the passage of time. Putting a timer on the plot speeds up the events to a high degree and forces player action. Someone betrays the PCs' plans to the corrupt sheriff so he can prepare an ambush. The stars are swinging through their courses strangely quickly, and comets are signaling that the Grand Conjunction might happen a week sooner than anyone thought. Cut time short, destroy crucial resources (a curse rots a scroll, a gifted set of healing potions turns to dust), and reveal that a bridge over a vast and demon-haunted chasm has been destroyed. Worse, key allies abandon the cause.

Make it clear at a critical point during your campaign that the characters are losing the struggle. People are abandoning them. Allies disappear—or swear allegiance to evil. Essential tools disappear, or entire cities are wiped from the map. The bad guys are winning.

As a game designer and as a friend, you might feel that making things worse and worse for the characters is ruining people's fun, is not sporting, and is going to make people dislike you or stop playing. This isn't true at all. Big challenges are more entertaining than little ones—if you play fair with the victories and rewards.

Being "unfair" and dragging characters through eleven shades of hell on their way to victory works only if the characters do, in fact, gain great rewards, find true help and keep a handful of loyal allies, and at some point have a difficult choice—but a real one—that can lead to a win. If the entire party dies before saving the world, you've gone too far. However, if the characters kill the demon-lord and save everyone, and then the entire party dies? Well, that might be just about right. In my perfect campaign (which has never happened, but there's always hope), the main characters all perish while winning the ultimate battle, and a handful of lackeys, henchmen, and underlings escape—to become the next generation of heroes.

JOURNALISTIC EXCESS

This technique is simple: Imagine the headline for each session of your adventure, then make it worse. "Rats Infest Hamelin" becomes "Plague Rats Infest Hamelin, Death Toll Rising." Likewise, "Miller's Wife Missing" becomes "Miller's Wife Lost into Elflands, Forest Expanding." No matter how bad the situation seems at first, the truth is more dire.

Here's the important thing about that embellished headline: You need to know it, but you don't need to share it in the opening hook. Keep it hidden until the time is right to make it clear that Things are Much Worse than expected. I find the headline technique helps me escalate my storytelling. And escalate it some more. And then, in a virtual special Sunday edition with color pictures, escalate it into the most horrific grand finale I can imagine.

To paraphrase Ron Burgundy, you might want to things to escalate quickly. You might want them to escalate slowly, but you do want them to escalate. A campaign might start with missing persons, but you always, always want the trouble to be bigger than initially presented. The missing people are slated to become human sacrifices, or they are enslaved to dig out poisonous stones filled with black mana. Worse, the missing people have been transformed into ghouls that fight against their former friends. Worst, their leader captured a beloved party mentor or henchman, and that friend returns to the heroes—planning to kill them all.

MAKING YOUR SESSIONS MATTER

Early on in your campaign planning, choose the elements that matter to you and make those things seem grandiose and larger than life. Courtiers wear lavish costumes slathered in jewels and illusions of gamboling rabbits. Weaponry speaks in ancient languages. Villains should be dark and dangerous. Avoid making everything "shades of gray" unless you are really, really committed to morally ambiguous plots. More often than not, big beats and an over-the-top tone will win you bigger fans than carefully arranged encounters of realistic tone.

Look at *Stormbringer*, look at *Lord of the Rings*, look at *Game of Thrones*—their tone is not meek and their style is part of their appeal. So as a storyteller, don't speak quietly, don't hide your most charismatic villains, don't skulk in the shadows. Or if you do, skulk so well that the PCs realize only later that their most secret council has been compromised!

A rewarding campaign needs someone willing to make creative changes and, frankly, treat characters (but never players) badly. Be bold. Be "unfair" to make each player victory sweeter, and be excessive to make each campaign all that it can be. Don't hold back out of a false sense of compassion or fairness. Drag the heroes through 20 miles of bad road, because every rotten reversal makes the heroes' saga even more amazing. Amp up the headlines and give heroes tasks worth the telling. No one, ever, cares about killing a bunch of sewer rats. Every hero secretly hopes those sewer rats are all secret servants of the Demon Rat-God, a foe worthy of their steel. Give them worthy larger-than-life foes, and your campaign will prosper!

BRANCHING STORYLINES AND NONLINEAR GAMEPLAY

Ree Soesbee

From the earliest start of roleplaying games, players have been given agency in telling a story—not simply listening to a tale, but being an interactive part of its unfolding. Choosing a path, solving puzzles, and fighting enemies are all part of the allure of a roleplaying game. However, with each choice the players make, the world changes. The GM must remain ready and able to adapt. Although a GM can prepare, you can never anticipate every change that the players will bring to the story, nor should you. Adaptive storytelling is on-the-fly, exciting, and fun, and it makes the players truly feel like the heart of the tale. Each decision the characters make modifies the outcome of the plot. Every action they take can change the world.

Interactive storytelling, such as that used in RPGs, LARPs, and even video games, offers multiple choices to the player. By accepting and acting on those choices, the player assists in crafting a personalized story. The challenge lies not with the player, but with the GM, who must keep pace with all the choices the players make—and the choices they did not make! The best way to be properly prepared is not to map out every possible option that the player might take, but instead, to create a living world with fully realized NPCs who have their own goals, perceptions, and motivations.

Nonlinear games rely on strong subplots, particularly through NPC motivation and setting (world) realism. You might not know in advance that a player is going to choose to throw a rock off a cliff, but you know how gravity works and can quickly adapt to the action. There is no "right way" to interact, and there is no "right choice" (though there might be a moral one). There is only player action and world reaction, combining to create change and (sometimes) narrative momentum.

LINEAR STORIES

Linear stories are straightforward. The plot and action move from point A to point B to point C, following a direct line of GM control. Such stories have advantages, such as the ability to foreshadow plotlines to come, and they present a cumulative effect of previous encounters. A linear structure can help a story feel like it has a defined beginning, climax, and end. However, those benefits come at the cost of player agency and player investment. Players are along for the ride, and it might be a fun ride, but the journey isn't uniquely theirs.

BRANCHING STORIES

A branching story, by contrast, allows a player's actions to cause definitive, measurable changes from the original storyline. These changes can take the story in countless different directions, and the GM must be ready for deviations both small and large. Multiple villains are possible, all with their own means of causing havoc, and the player characters' attention is more effectively challenged by multiple opponents. The players prioritize their characters' interests and responsibilities and pursue goals in the order they feel most appropriate, rather than following a scripted list of events.

Story branching encourages players to make distinct choices. Dealing with the results of those choices might cause players to make mistakes and recover from them, deal with ambiguous moral or ethical situations, and look for paths in the story that can lead to different outcomes. When players make choices and the story changes, they see the results of those choices within a continuing plot. Decision-making tests a player's problem-solving skills. It also tests a GM's ability to represent the game world on the fly, modifying the story to illustrate tangible choices and results.

SMALL CHOICES, LARGE RESULTS

Let's say that the adventure du jour is as simple as "the character finds an abandoned orc child." After appropriate research and preparation, you expect three possible outcomes from the player character: one, the character leaves the orc child to its fate; two, the character kills the orc; or three, the character takes the orc child to the nearest temple and leaves it on the steps. But what if the player decides to use magic to make the orc appear as a human? Or if the character adopts the child?

A GM can't prepare for every single possibility. Instead, you should plan as best you can and create a world that responds logically to character activity. Perhaps one of the PC's allies is a well-defined NPC magic user. When a character uses magic to change the orc's appearance, that NPC might condemn the character for using magic capriciously (or perhaps treacherously). Alternatively, the NPC might respect the player character for using magic creatively. If you have a good handle on the NPCs' stories and personalities, it will be much easier to respond to the unexpected—by seeing the events through the lens of the NPCs.

Giving the players agency means that the players invest in their characters' actions. If the characters' actions caused a plague, the players tend to feel responsible, and therefore interested in the situation. Perhaps they work to hide their role in the creation of this new disease, or perhaps they strive to cure it. Either way, the players' emotions are now tightly tied to the outcome of the choice, and the plot has more impact because it started with their actions.

THREE TYPES OF BRANCHING

The three most familiar types of branching stories are web, multi-terminus, and sandbox.

Web

The most common form of branching is a web. Players can make many different choices, leaping from strand to strand, but eventually all paths lead to a distinct central story point. Although this is technically branching, the central plot issue has only one answer, and no matter how the players reach that answer they must end the story in a specific manner or at a particular place. This allows the GM to control the climax and resolution of the tale.

You can build a series of "blockages" within this sort of structure, forcing players to check in with your planned program as their characters move through the game. Player characters make choices and their actions can be meaningful, but at certain choke points they must visit a certain place or perform a certain action to proceed. The plot is flexible, but it always returns to those choke points. From there, the players can again branch out, making meaningful decisions, but always returning for the next blockage in the plot.

With web-and-blockage story design, players believe they have free will and the plurality of choice, while they are actually being guided toward independent story points that exist regardless of their actions. That's not to say the choke points must be limited; each one can have multiple resolutions, and player choice can determine the plot as it progresses forward from that point.

You place clues throughout the world, allowing the players to locate them in any order and then put together the correct result from their findings— something possible only with a complete set of the clues, no matter in what order they are gathered or how they are retrieved.

Multi-Terminus

The more dynamic form of branching allows the players' actions to have full impact; to change not only the individual story point where the action takes place, but also to change the outcome of the story as a whole. Like a river delta, each branched storyline spills out into another potential ending. The endings thus created are individual and distinct. There is no "wrong" path. The GM is flexible and player choices truly affect the world.

If using this form of branching, the GM must be prepared for the players to fail. Not every outcome leads to a profitable resolution. Sometimes, the players' actions should lead them to ruin, or at least, to a less-than-beneficial outcome. The risk of such a result should prompt the players to think carefully about each action, knowing that no safety net exists to guide them back to a correct path.

A wizard's familiar has gone missing. The players might choose to ignore the plot thread, to start searching for the familiar immediately, to put the matter temporarily on hold while they attend to other tasks, or any of innumerable other options. However, until the familiar is found by the characters, it will remain missing, and the wizard who owns it will retain information critical to the player characters' story. If the characters retrieve the familiar quickly, the wizard is grateful and also offers to grant the players a spell scroll that might be important to their ongoing quest. If the characters delay in their search for the familiar, they earn the wizard's thanks but will not gain the bonus information, the spell. The story has changed.

Sandbox

In sandbox gameplay, you do not create an overarching story at all but instead invent a fully realized world, with complex and motivated NPCs and situations. This type of story design allows for complete player freedom. The world responds to the players' actions, without other intent or direction. The players create the story through their activities, interests, and character motivations. You must keep up with the players' choices and find ways to make them relevant and intertwined to form a story.

Sandbox story design can fail if player character motivations aren't strong enough, or if the world isn't populated with fully fleshed and individual NPCs. Most stories come from those NPCs attempting to fulfill their own wishes, and the player character blundering into them—for good or for ill. Certainly, this form of gameplay can open up possibilities that you never would have imagined. It can also result in an uninteresting game, if the choices being made don't have real impact. Further, it can too easily turn into a world without a story, without drive or significant plot, and that's no fun for the players. Player characters with strong goals of their own will have more success than players with relatively aimless characters.

When a player characters have strong goals, it is also possible to run an entire sandbox game based on those goals. NPCs can be designed and placed in the world to meddle with those objectives, causing a player to adapt to difficulties, setbacks, and challenges presented to them by the GM. Again, this relies on strongly defined NPCs with ambitions and logic of their own.

RUNNING A BRANCHING GAME

When a story takes a sudden left turn, you have a lot of options to keep the game "on track" or "in genre" or roughly consistent with your world's premise. After all, it's one thing for a story to zigzag based on player interaction, and entirely another for a well-designed world to be turned into farce because players found a loophole in plot, rules, or motivation.

Although a nonlinear game allows players greater freedom, it is more difficult for a GM to manage. Plots can fall by the wayside, and the game can feel undirected and sparse. However, a certain amount of branching is possible, and necessary, for the game to feel alive. Players need to feel invested. You can most easily accomplish that by allowing them free will to make choices, and then showing that those choices have solid impact on the world and the storyline.

A fully sandboxed game can lose direction and feel aimless. The GM should offer both linear and nonlinear elements, within a sandbox environment that adds to gameplay rather than diluting it. A GM who uses branching storylines must be prepared to give up a certain amount of control over the story, while retaining control of pacing, consistency, and plot. You can use gameplay to create a meaningful and emotionally charged story by building on the decisions of player characters, but it requires the game world (and NPCs) to be fully formed and self-motivated.

FULLY FORMED NPCS

Creating effective NPCs is a staple in a game that reacts and responds to player action. Fully formed NPCs are more than single-purpose characters, and they should have complex and long-term goals, unusual quirks, fears and loves, and an integrated place within the world. The more relevant these characters are to the PCs' story, and the more their prominent goals work in concert with their personalities, the more a Gamemaster will be able to utilize them to help (or hinder) the goals of the player characters— and create a more responsive world.

To begin fleshing out an NPC, write down one of her quirks, goals, fears, loves, and background experiences. This helps to frame her motivations, her directed purpose, and how she interacts with the world in the absence of the player characters. Knowing how the world moves without the player characters in it helps you decide how that world responds when the player characters' actions are integrated into ongoing events. If the NPC would have rescued the orc child, the player character saving the child instead might make her grateful—or jealous of the attention the player character receives for the action. The response is based on having a solid grasp of the NPC as a person, with motivations and fears of her own.

Each major NPC should also have a world goal—something too large to easily accomplish (or perhaps too large to accomplish without significant travail), such as becoming a king or discovering a significant spell that has been lost to the world. That goal transcends any lesser ambitions and embodies the hopes and dreams of that NPC. When player characters interfere with that large-scale hope, the NPC reacts more passionately than had the player character assisted (or denied) a smaller goal.

To fill in details about the NPC Mortimer Uthwyn, the Gamemaster decides that he likes cats of all kinds, plans to start a magic-users' school despite the city prohibitions against it, fears the reprisal of the priests of the God of Justice, and loves studying spells related to water. When he was a young man, he met a priest of a god of Justice who told him that liars had their hands chopped off, and now he has an unconscious quirk of pulling his sleeves down whenever he lies or feels nervous. He wants to meet a real dragon, and he gets very angry when people tell him they no longer exist.

OVERWHELMING BRANCHING

What happens when a story goes so far off course that you can't make a story out of it? Well, ask yourself this: Are the players having fun? If so, then let the decisions roll. Keep a careful tally of events, and after each session ends, use that tally to come up with a new story that evolves from those decisions. Can you pause and rewrite, salvaging some of the events you had originally planned by using them from another point of view? This is the flexibility I keep praising; it's a willingness to throw away cherished story ideas and start again.

Allowing players to have agency is good for the game. Letting them overwhelm your story with foolish decisions, destructive consequences, or not taking the game world seriously can be problematic. If a player abuses his ability to make decisions by making the game boring, offensive, or nonsensical for other players, talk to him. Reaffirm the nature of the world and his character's place in it, and ask if his decisions can more accurately reflect that story.

It might be difficult to distinguish between a world that is reacting to player character involvement, and a world that has gone off the rails due to player character action. Listen to your players and take their concerns seriously. Have a short downtime session whenever necessary and talk to them about the direction of the story so far. If your players universally express discontent, think about the direction of the world and how to get it back onto solid ground. If your players are having fun and still see the world as a concrete and realistic place, then their decisions are not negatively impacting the story of the game. Player feedback, and your own instinct, is key to understanding the difference between a flexible story and one that no longer has a solid basis.

CONCLUSION

Limiting player choice limits player investment. Build a solid world, and you can witness stories evolve from player characters interacting with that world. Don't be afraid to drop a preplanned story in exchange for one that occurs based on a player's decisions. As long as events occur naturally, allow the players to shape the world. Players are naturally more invested in stories they choose to unfold/start/instigate.

The story as you see it might not be the story that the players want to tell. Trust your players to make realistic decisions and encourage them to show you their characters' motivations, long term plans, fears, and desires. Use those to modify your intended storyline toward the results of the players' decisions.

CROOKED CHARACTERS

A Simple Guide to Creating Memorable NPCs

Richard Pett

The greatest *usefulness-to-dollar* (or in my case pound sterling) value of anything I've ever bought for roleplay has to be my first edition *DMG*—it is literally a firestorm of ideas and inspirations. Small wonder we waited so long for it at the time. She still sits at my side as I write adventures, her tables and ideas helping me out of many a tight corner.

There's a great resource in the book, spread over three pages and titled "Non-Player Characters" with the subhead "Personae of Non-Player Characters." It's crammed with aspects of personality—too much almost—everything from randomly generating alignment and moods through what an NPC collects. The tables remain amazingly contemporary and useful, and it's been the inspiration for many a crooked NPC I've had the pleasure to drag, kicking and screaming, into reality. The *DMG* forms a magnificent starting point for creating a truly memorable NPCs; I just transform them a little.

Working on a new NPC can be divided into constituent starting points using the method below—but do use this suggestion as merely a beginning. The best NPCs start with a kernel of an idea that grows into a rich crop in your own imagination and campaign.

THE TRAITS

First, use a d50 to determine an overt **trait**. Generally bear in mind the intention to create someone memorable, so go for it big time. Your secretively cruel NPC doesn't merely pull the wings off butterflies, she makes an art out of cruelty. She rises in the morning and goes to bed at night thinking cruel thoughts or reflecting on cruel actions past, present and future. If you prefer not to depend on a random roll, pick a trait to start from. As we'll see shortly, rolling for two or even three traits can also suggest interesting concepts; how many is entirely up to you, and opposing traits can make for even more fun NPCs.

If you prefer subtle, then tone these traits back to a level you're happy with and be sure to have a good spread of shades of light and dark.

Traits

1.	Aggressive	26.	Manipulative
2.	Angry	27.	Meek
3.	Awkward	28.	Melodramatic
4.	Belittling	29.	Merciless
5.	Capricious	30.	Miserable
6.	Charmless	31.	Moody
7.	Cheerless	32.	Narcissistic
8.	Compulsive	33.	Opinionated
9.	Cruel—overtly	34.	Outrageous
10.	Cruel—secretively	35.	Paranoid
11.	Cunning	36.	Pathetic
12.	Deceitful	37.	Pessimist
13.	Delusional	38.	Precise
14.	Dour	39.	Puritanical
15.	Draconian	40.	Racist
16.	Erratic	41.	Repressed
17.	Faded	42.	Scathing
18.	Greedy	43.	Self-important
19.	Hungry	44.	Self-indulgent
20.	Hyper	45.	Selfish
21.	Immature	46.	Timid
22.	Irritable	47.	Troubled
23.	Isolated	48.	Vain
24.	Jealous	49.	Vindictive
25.	Lazy	50.	Vulgar

THE CROOKS

Once you're happy, use a d50 again, this time to develop a **crook**—an overt aspect of that NPC. This is in many ways a physical manifestation of the trait and might suggest a reason or result of the trait in question. These crooks are deliberately broad in nature to create memorable NPCs. If you want to tone them down a little, come up with your own lists—once you get started you'll soon find they flow easily.

Crooks

1. Always seems to have an open wound or blemish
2. Attends to an imaginary parent and speaks to him or her loudly and often
3. Awakes at night screaming and falls asleep by day
4. Believes herself to be of royal blood
5. Believes one of the PCs is in love with her—and likes it
6. Believes one of the PCs is in love with him—and loathes the idea
7. Blesses everyone she meets
8. Can't sleep
9. Carries an imaginary baby
10. Collects something unusual, obsessively
11. Constantly attends to everyone else's needs
12. Constantly crafting—sewing or carving or baking
13. Constantly prepared for imminent Armageddon
14. Covers her skin when outdoors
15. Dances most of the time
16. Dresses in black
17. Dresses outrageously
18. Eats constantly
19. Finds everything hilarious
20. Frowns all the time
21. Gives money away constantly and is often followed by beggars
22. Has a bizarre pet she adores
23. Has a dark secret
24. Has a piglet/kitten/puppy and thinks it's a baby
25. Has a second—completely opposed—personality
26. Has an all-consuming passion
27. Is an obsessive artist
28. Is incredibly self-important
29. Is obsessed with another local NPC/club/family
30. Is obsessive about a PC
31. Is obsessively clean
32. Is often surrounded by an imaginary flock of small birds—usually starlings
33. Is often surrounded by one particular type of domestic animal
34. Is outwardly amazingly cheerful
35. Is passionate about something unusual

36. Is still in mourning for a long-dead spouse
37. Is very loud
38. Obsessively scratches
39. Prays constantly
40. Sees devils sitting on other people's shoulders
41. Sees her body as a canvas
42. Sings hymns obsessively
43. Smiles all the time
44. Speaks to the dead
45. Speaks with an imaginary friend in tongues
46. Talks regularly about his past lives
47. Talks to a glove puppet confidante
48. Talks to herself
49. Wants something desperately
50. Wears a mask

TRAIT + CROOK = NPC

Using our traits and crooks, we can create a starting point for our NPC. From the random method above you'll generate notions to work with and can move quickly onward from there. Remember you're trying to make an NPC for a particular occasion—not as cannon fodder. (Unless you want deliberately interesting cannon fodder.) The best NPCs have understandable motives (even when they are vile); this makes it easy for the PCs to comprehend their actions and makes them all the more memorable.

A DOZEN NPCS

Using this method, I quickly outlined a dozen NPCs. I literally gave myself 2 minutes for each one; it's good practice and fun to create a few NPCs so rapidly. Go with a method comfortable for you, though—if, for example, you like to mull on characters as I do with plots, then let the traits slowly sink in and play about with them.

After each name you'll see the random results I rolled, together with a quick take on how the NPC can be developed. These NPCs are created using one, two, or three traits and a single crook, but that's just one approach; try using others and seeing where they go. I've included possible uses for the NPC in question. Some might be obvious enemies or definite friends, but I've tried to give you a good spread. The gods of the dice guided me, and I made no adjustments to the rolls.

You'll see I've made no suggestion of race or class (except one, which I couldn't resist). As samples for you to use or play with, you should choose your NPC's background and adapt it into your own adventures.

When you've had a look at these suggestions, have a go at creating your own. Hopefully, if you find this chart a tenth as useful as I've found the 1st edition *DMG* section on NPCs, you'll refer back to it when you need a little inspiration in the future.

Happy characterizing!

One Trait NPCs:

Constance Willowbetter—Paranoid—Speaks to the dead: No wonder Constance seeks the PCs' help. The voices inside her head threaten her sanity, but is she an innocent madwoman or a link to something darker? Constance sees disturbing images lurking at the edges of her vision, and the messages come unbidden, appearing in her mind. Will the PCs doubt her like all the others she's tried to get help from?

Simeon Gribble—Cunning—Has a bizarre pet he adores: Simeon often speaks to his beloved chicken Mother Deception. He has a plan about to come to fruition—his chicken is brooding on six cockatrice eggs he's stolen, and when they hatch, he'll let them out in the farmyards of all the people who laughed at him.

The Maackallinally—Greedy—Believes himself to be of royal blood: THE Maackallinally had to leave the last town after it ran out of caviar, but on the trail he met up with a group of kindly strangers whose campfire he shared. He told them of his royal heritage—a knight fallen on hard times—and his hopes to reclaim his lands. He's sure he'll get their help, especially when he uses his cunning to manufacture a false deed of ownership. In the meantime he's worried they might see him steal the last boar rib off the spit, but can't stop himself—it looks so juicy.

Uriah Murkin—Melodramatic—Collects something unusual, obsessively: Uriah isn't popular, even in a city this big. He has to keep moving from house to house, which is not easy with his several swarms of wasps. Something very odd has happened today—one swarm started building a nest, and it's taking the shape of a human. Sadly, Uriah has told so many tall tales that people have stopped believing him. Perhaps he'll find strangers to help.

Two Trait NPCs

Qadeem Zh'in—Precise—Pathetic—Sees devils sitting on other people's shoulders: Even the nobles respect him as an artisan; no one paints miniatures and portraits like Qadeem. He might charge a fortune for his work, but he's so spineless that everyone underpays for his efforts. No one believes his stories about seeing devils on people's shoulders—after all, it's always those who have wronged him or owe him money. But when those people start to vanish, a restless lynch mob forms. Suddenly plenty of folk swear his paintings are coming alive. What do the PCs make of this event as they arrive in town and see a gallows being constructed for the poor innocent fool? Will they find the true culprit—a devil out to cause mischief among the townsfolk and take a few souls in the bargain?

Tabb—Pessimist—Compulsive—Is outwardly amazingly cheerful: He should never have struck the bargain with the giants. It's just that he loves Lilly so, and she hates him—he knows he's got no chance. So he made a deal with local giants for them to come to the edges of town while he creates a distraction and steals Lilly away. The giants can eat everyone else, provided he looks the big hero by saving his beloved—then surely she'd love him. Now, though, a bunch of strangers have come into town and they're readying to sort the giants out. Those giants are going to be pretty angry if they think Tabb set them up—and what if they tell the strangers about the plan. What is he to do? Smile as usual and try to think of something—oh, it's bound to fail, why does he do these things?

The Naff'irr of Ozram—Vindictive—Aggressive—Wants something desperately: Ozram is a proper baddie full stop. The Naff'irr has attracted a loyal if terrified following, and now they're camped outside of town with hostages. They want the townsfolk's immediate compliance. They want other things from the local kingdom too—things only people such as the brave PCs can fetch, so they are asked by the besieged townsfolk to deal with the Naff'irr. It isn't going to be pleasant. He wants power and wealth, so the PCs need to deal with his vindictiveness and aggression before the final showdown.

Zachariah Cockle—Faded—Hyper—Wears a mask: It all started with his level drains. He was never the same man after meeting the specters; they stole not only his energy but also his face, and now he has to wear a mask to cover his awful visage. Zachariah never rests in his search for vengeance. He scours the kingdom seeking brave companions to help him wipe out the wicked undead that created the spectres. His weakness might be his and their undoing, however, as he excitedly challenges the mightiest undead he can find—and he finds many of them.

Three Trait NPCs

Chastity Caddisfly—Cheerless—Lazy—Puritanical—Is an obsessive artist: Chastity is a difficult servant, but his holiness the high priest sees godliness in the imagery she paints. Now the priest desperately seeks help, because Chastity has fallen into a deep misery and taken to her bed. With the Grand Obiah of all the Church arriving in a week's time to inspect the ceiling of the Great Angelic Cathedral, the high priest seeks any means to entice the artist to complete her great work. But Chastity is impervious to love or common entertainment, so someone must find a new kind of diversion.

Young Lord Strangely—Belittling—Deceitful—Cheerless—Attends to an imaginary parent and speaks to him loudly and often: Taking on the role of lord after a truly great leader is not easy; everyone keeps talking about the good old days. So now the young lord has taken to consulting his deceased father in all matters and uses the imagined spirit's counsel to insist on his demands. Sadly he's no replacement for his father, and plotters are already eyeing the throne. Do the PCs side with the unpleasant but rightful heir, or do they seek to unmask his deceit before the royal court?

Tattletail—Immature—Pathetic—Charmless—Frowns all the time: Being a goblin is never easy, but being court goblin and high jester to Prince Porkling is plain misery. Are those frowns hiding a dark plot, however? The goblin makes a handy scapegoat for all kinds of subterfuge, and maybe in time the PCs see the goblin for what he is—a miserable and pathetic wretch, but no traitor.

The Great Wise Woman Mudgemerry Tanglegrim—Greedy—Troubled—Draconian—Carries an imaginary baby: The local hedge witch seeks a high price for her words. She has a hungry sweet tooth—just the one now—and has been carrying that "baby" in a scruffy shawl for nearly twenty years, never letting anyone see him. She provides words from the gods via her baby's whispers, and then she issues the most foul and rigid punishments and penances to all those who live in the vast and remote dampness of Galingale Marsh. None dare refuse her for fear of curses, although the villagers cannot abide her latest demand, which calls for everyone to move deeper into the marsh and supplicate her with sweets and gifts for her child.

FASHIONING THE ENEMY

Ben McFarland

Villains lie at the heart of any campaign. Dark, terrible forces, they pull the characters ever deeper into the story in a mad dash to stop their vile plans. Darth Vader cast a deadly shadow over a galaxy far, far away. The White Witch ruled Narnia. Sauron menaced Middle Earth. Loki threatened Asgard. Each one is iconic, with a distinctive demeanor and style. Villains generate the conflict to drive campaigns, and they provide the opposition that player characters struggle against throughout the game.

Your players spend hours contemplating how their heroes will develop over the course of the campaign, creating their personalities and capabilities. Shouldn't your big bad villains receive a similar treatment? Of course they should!

THE FIRST RULE

Even before you begin crafting the villain, before you consider anything else, you need to know what the villain wants to accomplish. This primary focus sets the tone for every decision afterward, because the scope of a villain's goal speaks to his or her ambition, dedication, patience, and even creativity.

The villain's goal should be very specific and expressed simply. This might be as straightforward as "claim the throne of the former Empire" or "rule the continent from the Black Ice to the Southern Deeps;" or esoteric like "replace all the heads of state with automatons I control;" or bloodthirsty and occult, like "perform a massive sacrificial ritual to ascend to godhood." The means to accomplish this task should already exist within the world, but your villain has the will to make it happen, either through his own actions or through the plans he puts in motion.

Success should be presupposed, because if the villain's goal holds a chance of failure, why would the heroes bother trying to stop the nefarious plot? Or it might already be accomplished, in which case the enemy wants to maintain the status quo. This goal will be the focus of the campaign's primary plotline, so make sure it's something you find interesting. If the goal is "maintaining the status quo," consider shifting it to a more active, "preventing factors and events that disrupt the status quo." In this way, you create a definite race between the villain and the characters, like Sauron trying to prevent the One Ring's destruction, or Queen Bavmorda from the movie *Willow* trying to find the baby Elora Danan. Once you determine the villain's focus, write it down. We'll come back to this goal later, when we think about adventures; now it's time to dive into the details of your antagonist.

OUT OF THE PAST

All villains begin somewhere, and their origins should influence them in a tangible way. Is he from a rural backwater, seeing poverty and lack of opportunity everywhere? Does she come from a cosmopolitan city, disgusted by corruption or the filth generated by living packed together— or feeling entitled to great wealth and power from birth? Maybe your villain was a refugee, who saw everyone precious die terribly and now hates the wars of indifferent nobles?

Consider Jadis, the White Witch in the *Chronicles of Narnia*, who had already destroyed the world of Charn and wanted to rule Narnia; or Darth Vader, the former slave who sought power to reclaim control over his fate; or Doctor Horrible, who saw the world as full of uninformed, inept people requiring firm command. The previous lives of each antagonist certainly shaped what they found valuable and detestable.

Determine the villain's homeland and how she spent her childhood. Where did she study? Was she a struggling apprentice, a disgraced student who taught herself, or a bright prized student? Who was the villain's mentor? Who taught her the skills she needed to become the future antagonist? Someone did, and you should decide if the instructor is alive or dead. Defeating a villain and discovering that her (possibly even more evil) mentor is still alive is an easy way to prolong a campaign arc, and a great twist.

This background provides details the characters can investigate later, perhaps discovering the information to find weaknesses, former possessions, favored tactics, or NPCs who can help understand the enemy better, just as learning Voldemort's origin as Tom Riddle helped Harry Potter understand the nature of the horcruxes. Utilizing these vulnerabilities, characters might find a villain's combat weaknesses, powerful spells that counter the villain's greatest strength, or insight into the scope of the villain's plans, providing an advantage they would not otherwise realize.

IN RECENT YEARS

Knowing where the antagonist begins is important, but most player characters will likely believe understanding the enemy's current situation has more immediate tactical benefit. You must determine where the villain lives. Has he established a lair, or occupied a stronghold? Does he command a personal dreadnought, or does he visit a circuit of cities in turn to monitor resources and recruit minions?

This lair need not be a static place. The Beast of the movie *Krull* kept a fortress that randomly teleported around the world with each sunrise. Syndrome from Pixar's *Incredibles* lived in an active volcano, while *Star Wars'* Boba Fett chased Han Solo across the Outer Rim in his interceptor, Slave-1. A memorable center of power or vehicle for a villain can effectively demonstrate the enemy's power, such as the ability of the Beast's fortress to teleport, or simply evoke dread and fear, as evidenced by the colonists fleeing the Cylon basestars in *Battlestar Galactica*. This base of operations helps define your antagonist as either a reactive enemy who waits for the characters to engage, or a proactive foe, constantly in motion and more difficult to predict.

Additionally, determine who employs your villain, or if he alone rules his domain. If there are powers behind your villain, how involved are they with regular operations? Emperor Palpatine regularly directed Darth Vader on specific missions, but the high priest of a cult dedicated to a dark god or captive demon prince likely receives much less exact direction—perhaps only vague visions or divinations. If this is the case, it adds ambiguity to the villain; is he truly evil, or is he simply a dutiful servant, unaware of his patron's true nature and willing to take any steps necessary to complete his missions? When your villain is the ruler, like Ming the Merciless from *Flash Gordon* or Dr. Doom from the *Fantastic Four*, it's important to establish who preceded them on the throne. Was he a usurper, or just another in a long line of cruel despots?

In any case, what are his responsibilities as ruler? Is he directly involved in ruling the realm, or does he maintain a capable bureaucracy instead, like The Lady of the *Black Company* novels? She built such an efficiently run empire, she could even leave it and join the Company as an officer. A villain who isn't distracted by the demands of leadership is a villain with more time to achieve other goals. However, a villain detached from the regular operations of his or her lands might not notice the characters' careful sabotage until it was too late.

WHAT HO, MINIONS!

On a related note, who immediately serves your villain? Does she keep servants? Is there a circle of trusted lieutenants like the Witch-king and

Black Riders, the Mouth of Sauron, and Saruman, who all worked with or for Sauron in the *Lord of the Rings*, or a single beloved adviser, like Jafar from *Aladdin*, Iago, or Captain Hook's Smee? You might provide a villain with unwitting allies who don't know the true identity of their master. These individuals might be turned against your antagonist by the silver-tongued heroes who bring evidence of the enemy's atrocities, or they might be impersonated to spy on the antagonist's secret plans.

Your villain's foes occupy the other side of that coin. The people trampled on the way to the throne, the family of the previous ruler and a remnant loyalist army, the displaced power players like the clergy of a rival cult who fled to nearby lands, or the conquered duke who wants his nation's freedom. These figures can serve as potential rivals or trustworthy allies to the player characters, depending on their natures. They might serve as grudging support in a pitched battle, only to turn on the characters when the villain's troops are routed. They might offer sanctuary and resources as the battle against the enemy's plans intensifies—some are surely mercenary enough to want to choose the winning side early. Knowing who fulfills these roles provides additional factions to your campaign and adds realism.

Finally, give your villain a couple of quirks, like a particular turn of phrase or an odd habit; a simple hobby, like a type of art, or a kind of puzzle, such as sudoku; and a few personal preferences, like a favorite food or a willingness to always stop to admire a kind of music or architecture. Your antagonist is a driven individual, pursuing a goal that might change or shatter the world; their interests shouldn't be overwhelmingly obsessive, but ought to clearly give them joy otherwise lacking in the world and people around them. Jame Gumm, the serial killer of *Silence of the Lambs*, raised death's-head hawkmoths, the *Avengers'* Loki is master of the snide comment, and the corrupt Chief of the Narcotics Division in *The Professional* had a love of classical music. These quirks can be exploited by observant characters to recognize the villain in disguise, or to identify when the villain has preceded them somewhere, or even to create a distraction that might delay the villain long enough to permit a vital escape or infiltration. They enrich the enemy's personality, making her more complex and interesting.

All this villain background serves the same purpose as a player character's background— it provides potential story hooks to investigate while discovering and thwarting the enemy's ultimate goal. But while the players have an inkling of the potential stories waiting for them in their characters' pasts and the GM might surprise them with those tales, the antagonist's background is a mysterious, tangled knot kept concealed from view. The party must actively try to find the threads comprising it, and dedicate time to unraveling it. The villain's history is, in essence, a hidden sandbox adventure in every campaign, waiting to be explored by the groups willing to discover it.

ONCE AND FUTURE DARKNESS

With your villain properly defined, reexamine the primary goal you established earlier. First, decide how your villain wins, how he specifically achieves his goal. Does he capture the five largest cities? Does he complete the incantation of ascension? Does he unleash the Spirit of Winter upon the land? By concretely defining the villain's victory conditions, you crystallize the manner of your campaign's final confrontation. Success shouldn't be a matter of the player characters' inaction, either. If anything, the final step should be an event that draws attention, if only to give the players one last chance at success. In the classic *Clash of the Titans*, the goddess Thetis announces the Kraken will destroy Joppa unless the princess is sacrificed in 30 days, putting the hero Perseus on a distinct schedule.

You should determine what the game world looks like if the villain wins. Will the villain leave the characters alone? Will they be seen as a continuing threat, or are they no longer relevant? What happens in the aftermath of the great plan's completion? If nations are destroyed or undead overwhelm the countryside, how does this affect the people and places the characters love? Write down answers to these questions, even if the answers are very broad, so you have some idea in cases where the party's fortunes go up in smoke, and the characters die in a heroic but futile struggle against evil. You can be sure the players will either ask you about the consequences or request that the next party take a shot at overturning this new state of affairs.

CALL TO ADVENTURE: BEGINNING, MIDDLE, END

Now, with the endgame defined and the portrait of your main villain complete, consider the arc of your campaign's adventures, examining the plan's foundation, machinery, and execution. Certainly, the villain won't dominate all the adventures, as player interests and character-specific quests occur in between events, but these elements provide the base plotline for you to weave other scenarios around.

Early Adventures: Lower-level foundation adventures involve the villain's acquisition of resources. These tasks are likely carried out by minions rather than the main antagonist, and they build on each other until the next tier of the plan is ready. This might include kidnapping all the weaponsmiths in the land to craft weapons for an army, seeking out ancient tomes used to research lost incantations, or infiltrating important organizations like a city's gate guards to easily capture a well-defended community. The careless mistakes of these minions offer inroads to the enemy's organization and hints toward the larger goals.

Mid-Level Adventures: At this point, focus on the machinery of the antagonist's plan, the elements that enable its completion. This might involve the construction of a super weapon's components, the acquisition and continued control of mystic ritual sites, or the creation of a powerful magical transit system allowing the enemy's forces to quickly deploy anywhere. Trusted lieutenants usually perform these operations, accompanied by an appropriately intimidating number of foot soldiers.

When the characters encounter these conspiracies, they learn much more about the enemy's overarching intentions, even if they fail to stop them completely. Plan on at least two of these missions succeeding in the villain's favor, both to show that failure is possible and to justify the villain's drive to proceed to the last phase. Build in multiple foundation and machinery adventures, emphasizing the complexity of the final execution. Consider foreshadowing the villain during the machinery phase, to expose the enemy's existence to the party and encourage investigation.

Red Herrings: For those GMs looking add another layer, consider including a red herring arc in the sequence, in which one of the enemy's lieutenants catches the party's attention in pursuit of an item or individual with little or no value to the antagonist's final goal. The true value lies in distracting the player characters. The plans might be complex enough that the players manufacture their own red herrings; feel free to chase these arcs through side adventures.

Additionally, if the antagonist becomes aware of the party's interference, the characters' families and mentors might become the targets of revenge. Why shouldn't the villain make things personal for them—it's certainly personal for the villain!

Finale: Finally, decide where the climatic execution of the villain's plans will take place. You don't need to plan the entire encounter—clearly, such design should wait until the game reaches the appropriate stage, so you can tailor it to the player characters, optimizing the potential fun of such a confrontation. Avoid the temptation to simply present the completion of the enemy's goal as fait accompli; while this technique worked in *Watchmen*, your players will have invested dozens of hours in the game and story, and they deserve the opportunity to attempt to defeat the villain's efforts.

Crafting an engaging villain is no small task. By utilizing these steps and incorporating a few episodic adventures exploring the party's backgrounds and interests, you can create a rich campaign, centered around a memorable and distinct antagonist while developing the player characters. A well-defined enemy and end goal help the adventures simply fall into place, easing session preparation and maintaining an exciting flow for the story.

PACING, BEATS, AND THE PASSAGE OF TIME

Wolfgang Baur

My friend Janice is not a roleplayer, because she describes the hobby as "15 minutes of greatness jam-packed into a 4-hour bag." And in a sense she's right: many roleplaying game campaigns are meandering, wandering, toothless things, with lots of tangents, humorous asides, and narrative dead ends. For most groups, I think that's part of the appeal. We all love those 15 minutes of greatness, but as gamers we're also glad to hang out, grind through some encounters, and tell a few fart jokes if we're playing the barbarian. All part of the package. Absolutely expected in the episodic campaign style. Not really a problem.

Sometimes, though, things feel tedious rather than leisurely and amusing. The pace of the game has moved from "slow but steady" to "nothing ever happens" or worse, to "OMG, I really would like to play something different this decade."

So we need to talk about pacing.

PACING AND PERCEPTION

Pacing is the art of keeping a game moving at the right speed for the players involved, and as a result is largely a matter in the GM's realm as much or more than the scenario design. The not-too-fast, not-too-slow happy middle ground is going to vary quite a bit for groups with differing play styles. However, I think that it's rare that people feel the pace is too fast. In most cases, the problem situations are ones where the game "feels slow." This can be the result of inexperienced players, an unprepared GM, a combat-grind-heavy scenario, or simply a misguided sense that the game's story elements must move at the pace of the slowest player. The sense that you are getting a few minutes action in an hour of play is what the clever designer and observant GM are trying to avoid.

We've discussed the feeling of poor pacing before, especially with respect to combat (see the *Kobold Guide to Combat* essays by me and by Jeff Grubb). To expand on that at the campaign level, let me just say that combat grind is, by and large, one of the greatest hidden enemies of a campaign's story elements. The other is downtime, and we'll get to that.

COMBAT AS CAMPAIGN WEAKNESS

Combat is the enemy of story because it provides such quick joy ("a crit!") at the expense of meaning and consequences. Many fights in an RPG are there just "to provide a challenge" or as relatively meaningless barriers to success. Combat is required for the characters to gain XP or plunder or to show the strength of the opposition, but in a larger campaign sense the fights don't do much. Yes, levels matter and individual victories matter. However, when the number of fights required and the length of time of those combats overwhelms the story elements of the game, the campaign-level material feels slow and players might complain that "nothing happened" even after the slaughter of dozens of foes in an all-night dungeon grind. There are no milestones of real triumph there; likewise, there are no memories of failure or loss.

Why is there so little sense of accomplishment during some nights of RPG play? Mega-dungeons contain fights and loot aplenty, but the poorly constructed ones fail to provide a larger meaning. An inexperienced DM can also fail to provide key moments and narrative thrust in a long-running game.

I believe that the arbiter of pacing, the sense of movement for characters and campaigns, is not combat but rather memory and narrative change. If a campaign is rich in battles but poor in memorable character moments, it feels weak and slow. If a campaign levels up swiftly but the world never changes, the sense of campaign pacing also suffers.

HOW TO SKIP AHEAD

The best campaigns don't allow the players to be the only ones setting the pace, and the best GMs likewise know when to skip large sections of story. Surprisingly few GMs feel comfortable saying, "the cult's agents escape you for months, until one day. . . ." This jump-cut technique gives a broader sweep to the campaign as a whole. It's especially valuable for blowing through weeks, months, or even years of downtime.

For example, years ago I wrote a *Call of Cthulhu* adventure called "Slow Boat to China" (unpublished). It involved a voyage across the Pacific, and I spent a lot of time figuring out what a passenger ship of the era might have been like, and what adventures our heroes could have aboard ship. And despite a dozen NPCs and three or four plotlines on board the vessel, the players burned through all the story beats before the ship got to Hawaii. What I should have done at that point is said, "You reach Yokohama a few days later, and then dock at Shanghai," as the remainder of the campaign was set in Shanghai. But I foolishly played it out day by day, and this made the pace slow to a crawl, because there wasn't much remaining of interest to heroic characters. The group was all expert roleplayers, and we had a good time, but for several weeks it felt like we were treading water (if you'll forgive that expression).

Sometimes, the easiest solution to a faster pace is just to say, "The next week/month is dull and passes quickly." The urge to simulate every day of a character's life leads to tedious games. Don't let your game become boring; tell the players that the group is skipping ahead to the good part. They might resist, especially if they have an ongoing daily habit of some kind. Tell them their task proceeds without incident, or you can handle it away from the group as a whole, but firmly move things forward to the next stage of the campaign.

Sometimes, the urge to "check everything" and "do just one more thing" becomes destructive to player satisfaction (and certainly to GM satisfaction), and your attempts to move the plot along fail. I'll point out that if the PCs are dawdling and examining ancient-but-worthless frescos, taking apart every floor, and spending days building a hydraulic acid cannon . . . there's no reason you can't advance the villain's plan without them. I've found that nothing spurs the pace of a campaign faster than news of a major victory by the forces of evil while the good guys were writing scrolls and sourcing silver ballista bolts. Make it clear to the party that the villains have accomplished something big while they were dawdling, and their focus will shift.

COMBAT AND CONSEQUENCES

You can also improve your campaign's pacing by dropping a lot of grind-y encounters from the play roster. I'm thinking here of the bandits, orcs, and low-level mooks of any stripe that show up to beat on the characters before the really important villains arrive—or that are completely unconnected to the main campaign storyline. Encounters can be clever and full of neat monsters and tactics, and still be sort of campaign junk food—they don't deliver anything new and they don't move the campaign arc closer to a conclusion.

I'd say it's OK to have some such encounters, because not every encounter needs to be about the main storyline. However, every encounter does needs to be memorable for it to contribute to a well-paced, moving, lively game night. If the only point of a combat is to provide loot and XP, then maybe that encounter isn't really carrying its weight. A better-designed version of that encounter would include an element of meaning that makes the combat memorable, a milestone. Consider the following potential additions to the combat:

- A villain's note or personal seal ring is discovered among the loot
- A body is found, a notable villager known to the PCs
- A character suffers a permanent loss of family, notable equipment, reputation, spirit, or body
- A character gains a new reputation, family connection, companion, or notable equipment
- The bandit chieftain pleads for mercy for her children
- The bandit priest pronounces a death curse
- One of the bandits is a fallen paladin, known to the party by reputation

Each of these elements might be a red herring or might spin off a major plotline. Or it might become "remember when we fought that bandit paladin?"—a moment that sticks in the players' memory of the campaign.

MORE BEATS PER SESSION

As a designer and a GM, your game is more successful when it makes a strong impression. So no matter how minor an encounter might seem, give it a story spin that reinforces the sense of events happening in the game world. Hollywood screenwriters refer to this technique as story beats, and video game designers turn to that tool as well. A story beat is simply an action that has consequences for the characters; they choose X, and so Y happens. They choose A, and then B happens. The characters' discoveries and decisions change what comes next.

The party delays and dithers, so the giants sound the horn of Ragnarok, and its echoes summon dragons. The valkyrie is disgusted by the berserker's crude remarks and abandons the party at the frost giant's doorstep. The paladin finds he cannot give up the raw power of an unholy weapon made to smite darkness. The wizard chooses to adopt a white cat with purple eyes, eyes that remind him of a youthful time. In each case, the character's choices have consequences and provide new avenues for the campaign. Some beats will go nowhere; that's fine, it was a moment, and in an improvisational medium like games some moments flash by without starting an avalanche.

However, over time, choices and actions build momentum. The necromancer who chose to traffic with dark spirits just once, for a good cause, finds that decision haunts his future choices. A good campaign takes each of these player choices and pushes them harder every session: The necromancer can choose to renounce darkness at the loss of combat prowess. The dark spirits can offer great help against even greater darkness, and so on. Eventually you build toward a full-blown story moment, where the campaign's choices lead to a decision point: either the necromancer embraces darkness utterly, or he is redeemed in some way, yet changed.

This isn't really about the character's statistics (though those will reflect the shift) as much as it is about the player's choices for the character. If the characters have the opportunity to make interesting choices and make them often, your pacing will be compelling. If the characters are not offered interesting choices and the story beats are few and far between, then your pacing will lag.

CONCLUSION

Humans love story games, novels, movies, and other narrative forms because they present characters who change. As a designer and GM, your job is to provide opportunities for change, for characters to show mercy and cruelty, for decisions to be made well or poorly, and for heroes to show great bravery and sacrifice—and for some of those sacrifices to be life-ending and remembered. To deliver great heroism, you need the story to move along faster than an endless stream of damage rolls, Python references, and pizza orders. Take command of the pacing in your campaign and stay one step ahead of the players with sharp new characters, nasty twists, and important story beats.

COMPLEX PLOTTING

Kevin Kulp

Your campaign is finally expanding beyond the first few adventures, the heroes are starting to gain power and prestige in the world, and you're ready to introduce them to the wonders of your campaign world. Your big challenge: a world, or even a new city, is ridiculously complicated. With every game session the heroes meet new supporting characters, uncover new secrets, and (best of all!) make new enemies.

How do you keep it all straight?

PLAYER ACTIONS CHANGE THE WORLD

Remembering to account for player actions is the best thing you can do for a long-term campaign, whether it runs five months or fifteen years. This makes tabletop RPGs different than computer games: what your heroes do each week creates significant ripples in the world. Those ripples change the world, for better or for worse, and the heroes are the ones who caused that change.

Your heroes slew Priestess Belera, a lawful evil church inquisitor who kept the city of Greenglass in icy lockstep with the state religion, and then the PCs headed off on a month-long expedition somewhere else. When they return, Greenglass is a different place. There's more crime, because petty thieves aren't being automatically executed; the PCs have become folk heroes to the local criminals, who scribble graffiti portraits of them on city buildings to annoy the temple; the temple now refuses to heal the heroes or support any of their causes; Belera's half-brother has arrived in Greenglass to investigate her death, and he's highly connected politically; and shrines to other gods are now appearing openly, when before they would have been mercilessly persecuted by the priestess. People have kind words or criticisms for the heroes, and they'll either buy them drinks or snub them in the local tavern. Either way, most NPCs have an opinion—and that's because the players' actions changed the city into something new.

WRITE IT DOWN

To put those ripples into motion, though, you need to remember what the actions were. The best method is a post-game summary emailed out to all players right before the next game, whether in outline or prose form. List everyone of note the heroes met, mention where they went, and summarize the important information they learned. Writing it down in a searchable form like email means that when you need long-forgotten details later, the answer is at the other end of a search box.

Organized GMs can toss everything into an online wiki, or reward a player with in-game or out-of-game rewards for handling this each week. Whatever method appeals to you, lean toward simplicity. The more complicated you make the process, the more often you'll forget or run out of time. If you keep it to a quick and consistent summary, you'll always have access to the information you need.

SEED YOUR GAME WITH ENDLESS PLOT HOOKS

You want multiple plotlines but you don't want to overwhelm your players. Go brainstorm five mysteries or adventure ideas that sound fun. Over a few sessions, let extremely generic information about these adventure seeds cross paths with the heroes. If they bite, great; if they don't, let them ignore it and slide the hook to your back burner—but don't let it drop off your list. Gradually, as heroes make new enemies and encounter new problems, add to the list of outstanding mysteries and plot hooks. Max this out at about fifteen; even you need to set a limit.

As they return to Greenglass, your generic ideas might include the following, introducing them slowly or in groups:

- *Belera's death causes political entanglements (good or bad)*
- *New priest seeks change*
- *Another town asks heroes to kill their hated inquisitor, too*
- *Belera's legal will leaves a haunted and cursed keep to the person who slew her*
- *You find Greenglass kind of boring without Belera, so an army of troglodytes are slowly undermining it from below*
- *The heroes learn that Belera was the old Emperor's great-great-grand-niece during the meeting with the new priest where they are told about the will; traveling peasants ask the heroes for aid, just about the time that they notice the town is smelling kind of bad.*

Plot hooks create change, and remember, change is good.

NEVER DO MORE WORK THAN YOU HAVE TO

If you're gradually seeding your game with five to fifteen plot hooks at any one time, you can't possibly develop all of those to account for potential player choice. Don't even try; you'll burn out quickly and be reduced to playing *Monopoly* while fondly remembering the good old days. Instead, have a general idea of the progression of those plot threads at any given time. They don't remain static, advancing with the plot as well.

Since hooks are essentially plots *in potentia*, if your players bite at them, you can interweave them into ongoing storylines or develop them in any direction you choose. If your players ignore them, you can either let them drop entirely—hey, other heroes in the world need adventures, too—or you can bring them back in later once campaign developments have made them more interesting.

Every time the heroes gain a level, mentally review your list of outstanding mysteries and plot hooks and think about how the changing world might affect that hook. If it'd be affected in a way that reengages the heroes, you can always introduce a clue about that in an upcoming game.

Political entanglements and a progress-minded new priest are slow-developing plot hooks you can save for later; you don't even pretend to do any development work on those. If the heroes accept work as religious assassins, you can have a series of on-the-road roleplaying and combat encounters before they reach the new town, so that will buy you a week to plan. If they choose to explore the cursed keep, you have that great map and adventure you've been wanting to use; and if they choose to investigate the stink, you can sketch winding tunnels on the fly as they encounter trogs. Perfect. Some of these situations will change or grow worse from week to week, but only the troglodyte incursion will quickly become obvious if ignored.

SLOWLY RAMP UP THE CONNECTIONS

The heroes might decide to find out why the trogs are angry, or they might wonder why that new keep of theirs has cursed them. Adding new plot hooks organically, as they spin off from already successful adventures, tends to be satisfying for both GM and players. Not only does it make the overall plot easy to remember, the players already have buy-in to each new adventure because it builds on past excitement and preexisting villains.

Your campaign becomes like a musical (jazz hands!). Each song (i.e., adventure) is different, but common themes wend their way through multiple songs, and the climactic finale draws multiple themes together all at once for a big coherent finish. If you introduce new music along the way that no one particularly likes, don't worry; it just never gets worked into the overall theme of the campaign.

USE VILLAINOUS ORGANIZATIONS

Never ever fall in love with your bad guys. I know, I do too, but they're only there to get smacked around by your heroes. To avoid a single point of failure in their nefarious plans, the best bad guys belong to organizations that share their long-term goals. They have mentors, sidekicks, lovers, and former adventuring companions who all act in the villains' best interest (at least some of the time). Use your weekly game notes to track what the players know of these organizations, and make sure your personal notes list who's a step or two above and below the main villain on the hierarchy.

Best of all, you can use multiple factions that have competing goals, any of which can side with or oppose the heroes. This lends the appearance of diplomatic complexity to any decisions the players make, and actions against one group might end up angering or befriending the others. Alter villains and encounters from multiple groups to make your encounter pacing more varied.

The late and unlamented Belera's connections include a snotty and politically ambitious half-brother; a spiritual mentor in the church who is as evil and uncompromising as she was; a somewhat cowardly assistant who will seize glory if it makes him look good; a heartbroken and vengeful wife who is otherwise quite a nice person; and a replacement priest who intends to cover up any peccadilloes Belera might have committed—even if he has to kill to do so. With so many NPCs to choose from, you only use the ones your players find most interesting or hate the most.

BEND EXPECTATIONS

To keep your players interested in a long-term game, consider a plotline, think about what your players will expect—and then defy their expectations by doing the complete opposite:

- The undead lich lord falls in love with the PC bard's music and does everything he can not to kill the heroes but to keep them safe so that he can listen to that music forever.
- The eccentric hat-and-staff vendor the heroes have run into a dozen times as comic relief is actually a transmuter who gets paid to permanently polymorph abusive spouses and bullies into leather hats, which he then sells at town markets up and down the coast.
- The sacrificial victim of the demon princess is actually the demon princess herself, imprisoned by a church of light a thousand years ago, and the wards have finally crumbled enough that she can be freed by a gullible group of do-gooders.
- Or perhaps the sacrificial victim is an angel with her wings sawed off, and the heroes need to race against time to stop the demon princess from being summoned directly into the angel's body.

You get the idea. The specifics aren't nearly as important as the goal: keeping the players (not the characters) on their toes by using surprise to regularly invoke their sense of wonder. And when you introduce a twist, write down your secrets in your GM notes so that you don't forget them before the start of the next game.

In addition, considering going big by raising the stakes. Let heroes change the structure of religions, of monarchies, of seemingly eternal prophecies. Let them be the heavy rock thrown into the placid stream. If the stakes of a fight include "the souls of everyone in the city" instead of "the rogue's going to die again, and we'll have to resurrect her," the battle suddenly becomes a lot more interesting.

BRING BACK OLD FRIENDS

Never make up a new friendly NPC—or dastardly villain—when bringing back an old one will do. Players love to re-encounter old friends from their first days of adventuring. It gives them a chance to reflect on how far they've come, to answer old dangling plot thread questions about hooks that you've since entirely written off, and to reminisce about that time a dyspeptic kobold almost kicked the wizard's ass. It makes the game feel homey. That's also true when you bring back NPCs who were once more powerful (politically, socially, or in combat) than the heroes, but who now are closer to peers.

Bringing back old enemies is just as much fun. To make this work you need an enemy who previously escaped, or one that can be brought back into existence without the players crying "foul!" One good technique is to change the form or the appearance of the reoccurring villain to demonstrate that the heroes' actions still had an effect—and to keep them guessing as to the returned villain's powers and abilities.

- The first time they fight the sorcerer Occitel, he has the appearance of an impossibly handsome youth.
- The second time they fight Occitel ("Hey! Didn't we kill that guy?"), he is hideously scarred and more physically imposing, some of his magic having disappeared as it tried to knit his broken body back together from nearby flesh, bone, stone, and steel.
- The third time they fight Occitel ("Dammit! Him?"), he is undead, a creature of malign will and shadowy magic who hates the heroes more than death itself.
- The final time they fight Occitel ("Oh no. It's him."), he's shed his body entirely and possesses the heroes' parents and friends, forcing them to find a way to defeat him without harming their loved ones.

If you want the villain to escape a few times with his life, find a plausible method to let him speak to the heroes multiple times without always being defeated. Methods such as astral travel, magical visions, disposable messengers, or mocking graffiti all work for this. The best villains come across as multifaceted people, not merely as monsters to be defeated, and as such you'll have the best success when you give your foes unique and memorable personalities that the heroes have a chance to discover through conversation.

You can also use this technique to reintroduce old forgotten plot threads that have interested you again, giving you a chance to tie your campaign's early and late adventures together into a satisfying whole. That's why you write plot hooks down, of course; there's no such thing as wasted adventure prep, because hopefully you can eventually recycle it into a completely different adventure at a later date and time.

Finally, did your favorite monster get killed in round two after you spent an hour statting it up? Reskin it and bring it back with a different appearance and different special effects, but the same combat stats. Everyone knows how to fight a beholder; a dozen elven revivified wizards flesh-grafted into a levitating undead golem, wielding magical wands even as all twelve heads simultaneously scream in eternal pain, might be a little scarier . . . even if they both have exactly the same stat block.

PULLING IT ALL TOGETHER

Great campaigns can last for a long time, especially if you have a rules set you love and a stable group of players. Games tend to grow organically, accreting more and more lore and trivia and campaign information, until even the most creative GM has trouble keeping it all straight. Using some of the techniques mentioned here, whether weekly game summaries or reoccurring villain organizations, will help you keep your game focused and streamlined enough to be as exciting as you want it to be.

And hey, that undead wizard née beholder? It freaked my players out.

SHARPENING YOUR HOOKS

Steve Winter

Whehen players and characters are fully involved in an ongoing adventure, a Gamemaster's job is easy. The GM might not know exactly which path characters will follow through the adventure, but the options are clear and all the GM needs to do is keep that adventure moving forward. Life is simple.

The situation becomes more stressful as the end of the adventure approaches and the GM hasn't communicated a sense of what might come next to the players. Aimlessness in an RPG campaign is as bad as dead air on the radio; if it goes on for long, people tune out or start looking for something else to do.

That's where adventure hooks come in. Good hooks get characters and players excited about the next adventure before it begins, so there's never a lapse in their engagement with the campaign. Improving your adventure hooks will make a big improvement in your campaign.

WHY USE HOOKS?

Use adventure hooks in your campaign for three reasons:

First, you want players to express interest in potential adventures before they start. Wrapping up an adventure brings a sense of completion. If nothing else is on the horizon, players can be tempted to leave the game. You can't end every session with a cliffhanger, but you can end every session with unexploited opportunities, unexplored paths, and unanswered questions still on the players' minds. No one wants to quit with unsettled business on the table.

Second, you want the world to seem like a living place. Real life never hits us with one problem at a time. We're forced to choose which problems we can deal with and which we must ignore. A world that serves up only one problem at a time feels inauthentically tidy. Even worse, it robs characters of the chance to make meaningful choices. Rather than adventurers carving their path to destiny, they become firefighters racing to the next emergency. Sprinkling hooks through the world makes the place seem real and gives players the all-important freedom of choice.

Third, proper use of hooks makes the GM's life easier. Your work goes into prepping adventures you know the players are interested in, so little time is wasted on paths the characters never explore.

ONE TECHNIQUE TO RULE THEM ALL

Fishermen have a saying: "It's not the hook, it's the bait."

The distinction is important. The term "hook" implies you're reeling people in against their will or better judgment, like a carnival barker pressuring suspicious rubes into a dubious sideshow attraction. It's much better to lure players with situations they'll walk into willingly, even eagerly. So we won't talk about ways to trap characters in corners they can't escape except by playing your planned adventure. Instead, give players what they want—or what they think they want, anyway. We'll keep using the term hooks because it's so rooted in the hobby, but understand that we're really talking about lures.

The very best technique is to sprinkle hooks into your gaming sessions early and often. Do that, and you're eighty percent of the way to mastering the art of the hook. The worst mistake you can make is to wait until characters are out of work and bored before dangling hooks in front of them. At that point, hooks all look like advertisements, and no one likes ads.

Hooks must arise naturally as characters move through the world on their business. They can be sprinkled into conversation at a roadside inn, overheard in the bazaar, whispered by informants or beggars, gleaned from wanted posters, found in the pockets of slain foes, howled in the night by creatures beyond the circle of firelight—and, yes, offered directly by prospective employers or their agents.

Crucially, most hooks should be bits of information characters either can't act on immediately or won't want to deal with at that moment. Instead, they're filed away for later, when characters have the time to tackle them. That's why this technique is so powerful. You don't need to have these adventures ready when you dangle a hook in front of the characters. You can drop multiple hooks, see what grabs the players' interest, and work on those.

UNTRUTH IN ADVERTISING

Let's say you have an idea for an adventure you'd really like to run. You cook up a juicy hook for it and run it past the players, but no one shows any interest. Scratch one idea, right?

Wrong. Hooks are basically rumors, and rumors aren't always correct. If the first hook doesn't grab the players, ask yourself why. Maybe it's too much like what they've done before, or too different. Maybe it sounds like a suicide mission, or a cakewalk (always a warning sign). The rewards might sound meager or unrealistically high.

It's the nature of rumors to vary from one hearing to the next. If you have a notion why the players weren't drawn to the first hook, let them hear it again, a little differently, a few days later or a few miles farther down the road. If it doesn't catch the second time, make adjustments and try a third version, and a fourth. Eventually you need to know when to quit—some frogs simply won't jump—but hearing conflicting stories about the same report in different places will intrigue some players. The more times they hear a rumor repeated, the bigger it becomes in their imaginations.

TRICKS OF THE TRADE

Dozens of "tricks" can enhance your hooks and make them more appealing. What works and what fails depends as much on the players as on the GM's selling ability.

Know what motivates your players. Gold, magic, heroism, power, acclaim, and excitement are the top drivers in fantasy games. Don't withhold the goodies! A hook must promise to deliver something the characters want. The more they want it, and the more of it, the better.

Leverage character bonds, flaws, and backgrounds, if your game has them. A hook doesn't need to appeal to every character. A strong appeal to a few characters' stories can be better than a weak appeal to many, especially if players trust you to eventually give everyone their day in the sun.

Avoid clichés and too-familiar plot devices. Where rumors are concerned, the more unusual and lurid the story, the more likely it is to be picked up and retold by storytellers and travelers. No one buys drinks for the person telling tales about a sick cow, especially if someone at the next table has a story about a talking carp casting enchantments on fishermen upriver.

Make it about people, not things. Even if your prospective adventure is about an object, such as retrieving an artifact, involving people makes the hook stronger. NPCs the characters know from previous adventures are excellent bait both as sources of information and as innocents threatened by dire peril. Ideally, they'll be NPCs who are useful to the characters; PCs can be astonishingly cold-hearted about innocent bystanders.

Put events in motion. In the real world, events keep advancing whether or not we intervene. The second time characters encounter a hook, it could be noticeably different because time has passed. If characters heard rumors that the forest king was gathering an army of giant spiders and ettercaps before spending five days exploring a dungeon, when they return to town they hear that the spider army has driven all the woodcutters from the forest and torched remote farms. A ticking clock is motivational, and as things get worse, heroes are more likely to take action.

Build on the past. Any time you can reference previous escapades in hooks, do it. Not only does that help to set the hooks, it also makes players feel that their exploits are known and their actions affect the world. The most powerful reference of this kind builds on the characters' mistakes: an NPC who died because the PCs arrived too late, or a villain who escaped because characters were searching for loot. What hero wouldn't jump at the chance to correct a past mistake?

Let players lead the way by providing key details. When they find a weapon in a treasure cache, ask its new owner to provide details for it based on his or her character. What's unique about the weapon? Whose family is represented by the crest on the pommel? Does it appear in any legends or curses? Once you have a player fully invested in that item, those details are sure to grab the player's attention when they crop up in future hooks.

Animals and natural events are more believable than people. Individually, people can be completely trustworthy, but as a collective, we're notorious liars. If animals or the weather start behaving oddly, then something's obviously afoot.

At the same time, don't overwork the omens. Oracles and portents are powerful tools, so keep them in reserve for truly important messages. They lose their power if they're overused. No more often than once every five significant missions is a good rule of thumb, or no more often than once every two or three levels in a *D&D*-style game.

Physical clues are more compelling than rumors. A treasure map in the hand is worth a dozen crazy drunks yammering about treasure in the hills.

Dying people don't lie. In reality, deathbed statements are no more reliable than any other kind, but they still carry special weight in our imaginations. An accusation made by a merchant who's dying from a goblin's poisoned arrow is especially persuasive, as are directions to the tribe's lost treasure when whispered by that same goblin with his dying breath.

Characters value information they had to work for more highly than if it fell into their laps. This is true whether the work was clearing fifty wraiths out of a crypt or roughing up a frightened goblin who surrendered to them. If characters believe they earned it, they'll put a higher value on it.

In the same vein, information can be delivered as payment for a service. A slippery patron might try the old dodge of, "Thanks for handling that dirty, dangerous job; I don't have 1,000 gold pieces to pay you, but I know where you can get twice that from a giant who's practically dead already." If characters are willing to go for that, the former patron will be sure to ask for a ten percent finder's fee!

Upset the apple cart. Don't be afraid to change the campaign world and leverage those changes as hooks. A town the characters visit often could be razed by marauders, a friendly shopkeeper could fall victim to a mysterious plague, or a baron who employs the characters could be assassinated and replaced with a doppelganger. The world isn't static, and social chaos is fertile ground for adventurers.

Also, create situations where the characters' actions can upset the apple cart by meddling in local affairs, as in the movies *Yojimbo* and *A Fistful of Dollars*. Like taggers with swords, players have a hard time turning their backs on the chance to spray their names on the world.

Inject a moral component. Circumstances can be constructed in such a way that, whether characters choose to intervene or to ignore the situation, they're making a moral choice. These situations are great for roleplaying because players find themselves in an interesting bind either way. For example, an NPC who's been a good friend to the characters and provided them with invaluable aid or information might be revealed to have been an infamous torturer for the despotic kingdom next door, before its king was overthrown. If characters help to shield the NPC from bounty hunters, they're protecting a war criminal; if they hand him over, they're betraying a friend who, to the best of their judgment, has repented and risen above his ugly past.

EMERGENCY MEASURES

Sometimes, despite a GM's best effort, a hook won't take. What can be done when a beloved quest is ignored?

Let it go.

If no work has been invested in the adventure beyond devising a few hooks, then nothing is really lost. Maybe players aren't ready yet or suspect they're too low level for the challenge; set the idea aside and bring it back in six months or a year. Maybe the idea wasn't half as good as you thought it was, and it deserves to be discarded. Never get so attached to your own ideas that you can't cut them adrift.

If you've promoted this quest as a major event in the world but players turned up their noses, then let it move ahead without them. If characters ignore a "this will only get worse" scenario, then it gets worse. That's the beauty of a sandbox campaign; the world has a life of its own, outside the circle of the characters' actions. Eventually the situation will become so dire that characters either choose to get involved, or another group of adventurers will step up and win the glory and rewards—and wherever the PCs go for the rest of their days, they'll be considered second-class heroes.

If you bought a big, packaged adventure and characters aren't biting on its lures, consider starting somewhere other than the beginning. An adventure doesn't necessarily need to start at chapter 1. A mega-adventure such as *Hoard of the Dragon Queen*, for example, could begin with episode 1, 2, 3, or 4. If hooks for chapter 1 don't work, wait a session or two and then drop hooks for chapter 2, using all the techniques covered above.

Being a top-notch GM is a craft. Like any craft, it takes practice, and the more you practice, the more proficient you become. Where adventure hooks are concerned, more is definitely better. More hooks make the world seem more alive, give the players more options to choose from, and allow the GM more opportunities to learn what excites the players. Drop plenty of hooks, drop them early, repeat the ones that get attention, and you'll have players who are excited about what lies ahead.

THE ART OF LETTING GO

Zeb Cook

It's time to imagine something inconceivable.

A GM sets out to run a game. He's good with stories. He knows how to create a good plot—maybe he's even had fiction or adventures published. Carefully taking his time, he works out a great adventure. The plot is intricate and exciting. It has all the right elements; a unique plot with twists and turns, big moments of action, clever puzzles, NPCs who aren't stereotypes, and a believable villain. The GM is happy and confident. He's prepared. He knows all the steps of the tale, where the players need to go, all the NPCs they will meet, and when to spring surprises on them. He can't wait for the players to discover all the surprises he's got in store for them.

And by the end of the first night, it's all a shattered mess. First the players refused the summons from the king, so he was forced to send guards to arrest them. The group was singularly unimpressed by the prospect of finding the king's missing mage, even though the assignment was obviously going to lead to greater adventures. They stubbornly grumbled when all the townsfolk they talked to had nothing to share except rumors. They ignored the intrigue the finely crafted NPCs tried to drag them into. They took an instant dislike to a pivotal character and wanted to rob him instead of talking. They particularly didn't like the heavy-handed guards sent to prod them on their way—and make sure they didn't cause any trouble in the process. By the end of the night they were darkly muttering the dread word no GM wants to hear: "Railroaded."

Sadly, if this sounds familiar, it's because this scenario plays out too often. So what went wrong? Why do good stories come to bad ends? Quite simply, the GM forgot the great unspoken rule:

Narrated stories are not games and games are not narrated stories.

This might seem like nonsense. Every great game session has a great story. And all those adventures people write, publish, and play have stories. But adventures make use of very different ways to relate stories. Different ways require different tools. Take the distinctions between books and movies. Stories in books describe how characters think and what they feel. The world is created through description that builds a picture in the reader's imagination. Movies have a hard time putting the viewer inside a character's head, so they change the rules for telling stories. There's no need to describe the world when it's right there on screen. Movies show stories—they show what people do, show what happens next, show the world. Bad movies describe what happened. Good movies show it happening.

And games? Games neither describe nor show. Games enable the players to tell their own stories.

THE WRONG TOOLS

So it's no wonder things went wrong for the earnest GM; he was using the wrong tools to tell his tale. The carefully laid out plot, the detailed character descriptions—these are the writer's tools. These tools don't account for the biggest difference between stories and games: the players. The players in a game aren't passive viewers. They don't sit still to be told a story. They don't act parts in a story. They take part in *creating* the story. Quite simply, characters take actions. Those actions become the story of the game, not the plot the GM initially created.

So how is a GM supposed to tell a good story when he's not in charge? What if the players go off on a tangent? Refuse to follow the carefully placed clues? Or, god forbid, decide that what they want to do is more fun than what the GM has meticulously planned? Giving up control is a scary prospect for many GMs—but it doesn't have to be. Fortunately, letting go doesn't mean cutting the GM adrift without tools or techniques to guide him. Gaming might not be the same as a book or movie, but that doesn't mean it can't borrow and repurpose their storytelling tools.

One of the best media tools isn't a careful plot outline or detailed character backstories. It isn't the filmmaker's script or storyboards. No, one of the best tools a GM can borrow is an actor's tool—the art of improvisation. That's right, those improv comedy and theater groups offer useful strategies for GMs to follow.

RULES OF IMPROV

Improv has rules? More like guidelines, the actors might say.

It's about trust. The GM needs to trust the players. The players are not the enemy or competition to be beaten. Likewise, the players need to trust the GM—that he won't be arbitrary, isn't out to get them, and won't force choices on them.

Setup is everything. To inspire action from the players, there needs to be a scene to react to. Don't say, "You walk into the tavern. What are you going to do?" There's nothing to work with there. Instead try, "You walk into the tavern. Everybody stops talking and three big guys turn to glare at you. The innkeeper squeaks and ducks behind his bar. What will you do?" The sudden silence and the glaring thugs are great hooks, concrete elements to react to. That's what a setup is: an invitation to do something.

"No" is the enemy. The old saw "There are no bad ideas" is true. Telling players, "No, you can't do that," is a game killer. Everything they propose is an idea, a jumping off point. They want a map to the dungeon? Have them buy one off a sketchy character in a tavern. Is it a good map? Or one that's going to lead them into trouble? When a player acts on an idea, they are making a choice. Just as the GM creates a setup for the player, the players can create story for the GM to react to.

Listen. Listen to the players. What do they expect? What do they think is the worst that can happen? More often than not someone will speculate about a horrible, awful doom that might be lurking just around the next corner. Listen and build on what they say.

Do, don't say. Once a scene gets going, keep it driving forward by ramping up the action, drama, or comedy as appropriate. Throw in complications and unexpected changes. "Suddenly the city watch bursts in as the tavern fight is in full swing. They are arresting everyone in sight. Now what do you do?"

Have fun. This should be obvious, but it is easily forgotten. The GM and players both need to enjoy the game. If that's not happening, switch gears.

TRANSLATING RULES TO ADVENTURE

Advice is all well and good, but turning ideas into something playable requires sitting down and doing the work. Just as playing a published adventure means reading the narrative and making notes, running an improv adventure means planning in advance.

It sounds counterintuitive, but preparation is essential to a successful improvised game. Think of it like filling up the tool box before building a house. If work has to stop every time a new tool is needed, the house will never get done. Preparation is about assembling the tools needed to run a game smoothly so there's no need to stop every time an encounter occurs. At a minimum, the GM should prepare the following tools.

Rules. This might seem obvious, but the most important tool is a set of rules the GM is comfortable with. If everyone is trying to learn how the combat system works, nobody will have time for anything else. Use a system that fits like a glove so the rules bend to the hand underneath.

A crib sheet of monster stats. Whatever the level of the adventure, take the time to create a list of monsters that might appear. You need only the basic stats to run an encounter. Noncombat abilities are unimportant—unless they are a prelude to combat. Knowing a monster can predict the weather isn't important. Knowing that it can predict player intentions is critical. Have this crib sheet handy when running the game, because having to stop to work up stats will ruin the spontaneity of the game session.

Stock characters. Likewise, it helps to have a few standard NPCs prepared and ready. These include guards, peasants, the traveling merchant, the egotistical nobleman and his retinue, tavern toughs, and whatever else seems like a good idea. Give each a few words to define their personalities (prepare their characters, not their rules). And don't forget to give them names. Again, don't worry about unimportant stats. In many cases stats won't be needed at all.

Questions for the Players. This is the big one. These questions will provide the raw material for encounters in the game. Basically, the players will be setting up many (or all) the things that happen to them, based on the answers they give.

THE QUESTIONS

At the start of the game, ask each player to give their character's answer to the following (suggested) questions. Let everyone hear the answers. Short of being hopelessly out of character, there are no wrong or bad answers. Smart players will figure out that this information will be used in the adventure and might purposefully give silly answers. That's fine; bogus answers can lead to good results, too. Remember, no is the enemy. Be sure to make note of who answered what. It will be used for and against them during the game.

As players give their answers, the GM needs to think, "How can I work this into the game?" By the time the players have finished, the GM should have at least one or two ideas for encounters. This is the point where the GM starts to create the setups he will later use.

Although ten questions are listed below, don't feel limited to these. Come up with new questions if these don't work. Nor is it necessary to ask ten questions. The goal is to gather material. Once you have enough material, there is no reason to pose any more questions.

Ten Sample Questions (with recommendations)

1. I really wish I had learned _____.

   (This answer is good for puzzles, traps, challenges, and confounding the characters with their shortcomings.)

2. My parents always wanted me to be a _____.

   (Use these answers to provide a bit of roleplaying for running jokes or situations where that's the talent/person the situation needs.)

3. My best asset/skill is _____.

   (What a player thinks is a character's best asset might not be true. Create situations that test their capabilities to the max. Nothing beats heroic success or failure.)

4. I would be most embarrassed to be killed by _____.

   (This question is a comedic goldmine, if nothing else. There should be at least one encounter that matches somebody's answer.)

5. My greatest fear is _____.

   (Of course this answer should be sprung on an unlucky player, preferably one who will roleplay the situation well.)

6. _____ would be awesome!

   (This one has heroic moment potential.)

7. The last thing I want to meet on a dark night is _____.

   (Boss fight!)

8. My goal in life is _____.

   (This is a good one to tease players with, as they almost succeed in attaining their dreams but complications ensue. For example, the character who wants to get rich keeps having fortune slip through her fingers, and the character who wants to be noble keeps landing in situations where the only outcomes are terrible or scandalous.)

9. I really hate _____.

   (This can be used for anything: an encounter, a complication to another encounter, or an NPC who embodies that answer. Again, the GM should encourage roleplaying.)

10. I want to be remembered as _____.

    (Always good on a headstone!)

Remember, this is not a hard and fast list. GMs should feel free to create different questions that better suit their players or the situation.

Finally, not every answer will be used in the game session. GMs should not try to force them all into a game. Particular answers will be clearly better than others. The right moment might never come up to use the prompt. This is fine. Remember that pacing is an important part of improv. Stories (and jokes) need space to be told. The GM needs to make sure the game stays focused and that everybody is engaged. Don't focus on a single player. It's more important for everyone to have fun than for every idea to show up on the table.

DO, DON'T SAY (REDUX)

Clearly, improv games work better in certain situations than others. Generally, they lend themselves to comedy better than tragedy. Once a humorous situation plays out, the group can move on to the next encounter without much concern for continuity. Drama requires more tracking of events to build a story over time. Dramatic improv can be done but it takes more effort on the part of the GM.

Finally, improv games can seem intimidating to run (and play) at first. Playing without a net is not simple. So while any article of theory and advice can simply to call it good and walk away, it is more helpful to translate advice into action. One of the rules of improv is Do, Not Say. All the advice won't help without a framework to practice on and learn from. To that goal, the adventure included in this book, "The Journey from Here to There" is a sample to help GMs test out the ideas given above in a real game session. After all, the best way to learn is by doing—and letting go.

PLOTTING A GENERATIONAL CAMPAIGN

Ben McFarland

Long-term games mean time must pass, and the setting will transform. Regardless of the time spent playing in the real world, the course of the campaign can take place over many months or years of game time. For example, I played in an *Ars Magica* game set in Mythic Europe from 1153 AD to 1163 AD over the course of seven real-time years. Occasionally, no time would pass between sessions, but when we completed adventures, anywhere from a season to three seasons might pass. In a different campaign, we ran the initial adventure over a few sessions, establishing the base of operations, and then jumped ahead three years of game time.

We see the long-term game implemented in video games, too, with the publication of titles like the *Fable* franchise, which occurs over the life of the main character and his descendants, sometimes allowing decades or centuries to pass, or the *Mass Effect* series, which takes place over the course of three years. Compare those periods with a game like *Halo: Reach*, which takes place from July 26th to August 30th. A long-term campaign can help you tell a richer story.

LONG-TERM GAMES TAKE WORK

Don't get me wrong. It's a labor of love, but anyone who tells you it's not work is lying. The preparation necessary for a successful long-term game, one where substantial in-game time will pass during the course of play, is fundamentally different from the usual campaign advice. Twenty years of handbooks and magazine articles and blog posts say you should start small and build the setting outward only as you need it. For short-term games, where the passage of time is ignored entirely or has no real importance, that style of preparation and development works extremely well. But multi-year or decade-long games require solid foundations, or you can easily find yourself contradicting information you gave the group from session to session.

Why go to the trouble? Because it's tough for players to become immersed and invested in games when they can't trust that their view of the game world is reliable.

MINIMUM REQUIREMENTS

So what does it take to create a long-term game?

Plainly, you've got to know the world and what's going on in it. But how do you go about creating a game environment that effectively supports this passage of time?

Start by deciding how much time you want to have pass over the course of the plotline and how far into the game future you'll be planning. If the duration of the game in real time is open ended, then you need to think about the amount of time that passes between adventures, and decide on how long your initial plans will cover. A year isn't a bad place to start. If you're planning on a campaign that covers five years of game time leading up to a massive event, then you might have variable periods between adventures, with anywhere from a few weeks to a couple seasons passing between adventures. In any case, I recommend creating a timeline on paper, to keep track of events. Mark each period, and then you can add individual events as you progress. Additionally, make copies of this blank timeline before you start, in case you run your campaign beyond your initial plans.

Next, create or use a solid setting foundation. You need to have a good sense not only of the local area where initial adventures will happen, but the larger surrounding region. This means being aware of the geography and the landmarks and knowing what kinds of natural events might occur, because those events ought to happen. Weather should be a part of a long-term game, since more than anything else, it helps mark the visible change in seasons and the passage of time. Your time line should note where Autumn, Winter, Spring, and Summer happen, to remind you to incorporate descriptions of the weather into the background.

Additionally, familiarity with the local geography allows you to know where earthquakes, volcanoes, floods, tsunamis, tornadoes, or possibly "just" immense amounts of snow might occur. Natural catastrophes can seriously alter whole regions, and you should use them very sparingly and treat them as purposefully chosen story elements. Think hard if you want those events to take place and then determine exactly where geographically and when on the timeline such phenomena are going to strike. When a volcano erupts, it's critical to know if the characters are hanging out at an inn in Pompeii. Sure, there's an interesting story to be told in the escape, but you're also wiping an entire city from the map, which changes the relationships associated with that city.

Those relationships make up the third task needed for long-term games, and relationships require people and organizations. As the GM, you need to identify the big players in the region: the rulers, the guilds, the nations, the cults, the movers and shakers in the overall sociopolitical structure. You need to have an idea of the history that created the current situation, but you don't need the full details, and it's actually better to leave the facts vague. By leaving the history only partially defined, you can later customize details to better suit the adventures. Your geographical map can help define a number of these important elements.

It's not necessary to outline too many details of these foundational events until your party needs that information. If you've decided that the city was shaped by a trade war, over the length of the game the players and circumstances around that historical event can be modified to suit the campaign. Trade might have been disrupted by a jealous prince who wanted to marry a bishop's illegitimate child who turns out to be a relation of a party member—or any other connection that brings the story closer to home for the party. You don't need to explore this level of "secret history" at the start, but that the details can develop during play.

These kinds of relationships provide an excellent reason to use an established campaign in this sort of game, since it reduces the necessary workload for this aspect. You can simply take notes as you read the text, instead of creating everything whole cloth. Or if you prefer, map your fantasy realms to real-world medieval country equivalents. A city-state of merchant oligarchs draws from Venice, while a declining empire beset on all sides is modeled after an aging Roman Empire based out of Constantinople. You don't have to stick to the established history in either case; the source material provides a baseline status quo, and the actions of your players might change your game world.

RELATIONALLY SPEAKING

With the important players and organizations established, the next step requires the GM to define the large-scale relationships between them. Who trusts and distrusts whom, who hates the others, who has fostered revenge in their hearts for nearly a generation? Who is allied to whom, why are they allied, and how much do they trust their allies? Is it an entangling alliance that requires a response from all allies when a hostile act taken against one group, or is it a false alliance where one member is waiting to betray another when the moment is right?

I prefer to relationships between entities that revolve around a resource or a person, and the relationships might not always be positive. For instance, two baronies have an indifferent attitude toward one another because little trade passes between them. There might be several reasons for the diminished trade, like goblins in a forest or bandits in a mountain pass, but you don't need to define the details right away.

Answers to these questions allow the setting evolve over time, as the characters impact the world around them. When it comes to these relationships, I recommend a policy that states, "Change no relationship unless the characters or the story interact with it." A long-term campaign involves many moving parts, and by leaving larger relationships static unless the characters or the consequences of the characters' actions change them, you minimize the change to the political landscape from season to season. As you become more comfortable with campaign events that unfold over in-game years, you might decide to make all the relationships dynamic.

ADD PLAYER AGENDAS, FRIENDS, AND ENEMIES

With the larger political relationships defined, you can take the backgrounds of the player characters and tie them into the NPCs of the region. Ask for short backgrounds from the players, perhaps as little as a paragraph. It should address the character's family ("Are they alive, how big are they, do they live in an urban or rural area?"), their instructors or mentors ("How did they choose and gain training in their class?"), any former or current loves, and their hobbies or interests, which might be reflected in their skills.

Yes, you're going to want to know their hobbies. In a long-term game, downtime happens. By knowing a character's hobbies, you can better describe what they might be doing between adventures, or even create adventures that cater to those tastes. Just as you need to create relationships for the regional entities, you want to build connections between the player characters and at least a couple of NPCs. This means both the good and bad sides and how they interact.

If you prefer, ask the players to suggest two friends and two enemies or rivals. Make sure to leave yourself space to expand over time, since nobody knows everyone, and these links can help create social adventures when your campaign progresses further. Additionally, you might need to address certain player expectations. People accustomed to years of short-term games could expect immediately results or acquisitions. Long-term games should reinforce a delayed gratification mentality.

ADVENTURES!

With everything prepared, it's time to create the adventures to take place in this setting. These might be a combination of short and long story arcs, and related or unrelated plotlines. Standalone pieces, like a dungeon delve, shouldn't extend beyond the current, single time period, be that a month, or a season, or whatever you've decided. Other events, like the hunt for a pirate queen, might take place over two or three points. Long-term stories, like the defeat of a coalition of giants and dark elves, should stretch across multiple time periods, possibly with several stories occurring in between. This presents the characters opportunities to research powerful foes or develop special items or magic to address problems, and gives the GM the chance to have "surprise" enemies appear to exact revenge, take advantage of a random encounter, or have a villain advance preparation toward a larger plan.

You should mark when each of these adventures occur on your timeline and indicate what relationships each might affect if the characters succeed or fail. For instance, if the characters deal with the goblins in the forest, I'd note success means trade increases, while failure increases tensions and lays the groundwork for a war to develop between the two baronies. The extended period between adventures allows a feasible period for your villains to develop lieutenants or alliances, and to shift their locations to create adventures in unexpected settings. You can drop hints through rumors and traveler's tales, taking advantage of the long-term campaign's "slow reveal" style.

SEASONAL REPETITION

Finally, a long-term campaign style means being able to utilize elements that add to the verisimilitude of the world while offering opportunities for interesting roleplaying and events. These include seasonal holidays, travel, and the creation of families. Holiday gatherings and events can present great backdrops for encounters or adventures; consider cultural events like the Running of the Bulls in Pamplona, or the two-day Hindu Festival of Colors known as Holi. These kinds of gatherings make adventures more memorable by adding unusual NPCs or events to what might otherwise be an urban investigation or simple trip for supplies.

As time passes, romantic plotlines become more feasible through the family and friendly relationships provided with the character backgrounds. Because the party members engage socially with NPCs over time, characters can establish families and participate in social life events such as weddings, funerals, and birthday celebrations.

In the end, the whole table benefits from the long-term style of play, since it provides better opportunities to become deeply invested in the campaign world, and it offers a living, breathing setting that changes with each story arc. Certainly, more work is involved in the preparation and execution of the game, but once it's moving at a full tilt, I find this kind of game much more rewarding.

USING CLIFFHANGERS EFFECTIVELY

Amber E. Scott

"Your time has come, evil one!" shouts Matthius, brandishing his holy avenger at the skeletal figure floating near the domed ceiling.

Aleemadra sneers at the adventurers standing beneath her. "You are even more foolish than I thought. For all your clever planning, you have walked right into our trap."

"Wait, what does she mean 'our trap'?" asks Kalendi the sorceress.

"And that's a good place to stop," says the GM with a grin, as a chorus of groans erupts from the players. . . .

Cliffhangers end a unit of storytelling (a film, a novel, a chapter, a television season, or a game session) on an unresolved dramatic note. In *The Perils of Pauline*, a popular silent film series, the end of every installation saw the titular character placed in another situation from which there seemed no escape—surely this week she'd be killed at the hands of a mustachioed villain! That sense of danger kept audiences enthralled.

Using cliffhangers in a campaign can ramp up the tension of an adventure, if used properly. Cliffhangers leave players pumped up, ready and excited for the next session. They spark imagination and give players the opportunity to wonder and plan. Used poorly, though, cliffhangers can have the opposite effect. Badly placed cliffhangers can frustrate, confuse, or bore players.

Fortunately, a few simple tips make it easy for any GM to use cliffhangers appropriately.

DELAYING A BATTLE

When the PCs finally enter the final chamber of the dungeon and find their long-sought enemy awaiting, it might be tempting to end the session there. The anticipation of waiting to face the ultimate antagonist can work, with a few preparations.

Careful Bookkeeping. If you stop the adventure right before the last encounter, it's important to keep track of where the PCs are, what spells and effects they have active, their hit point totals, and other minutia of their character sheets. Nothing will kill the drama faster than a 20-minute discussion at the start of next session trying to remember where everyone was standing and if the party has any healing magic left.

Smartphones or cameras can be a big help here. Snap a few pictures of the battle map and miniatures before cleaning up and then reset the table before the players arrive next session.

A master list recording the PCs' current hit points and active effects can help everyone jump back into the action as soon as the next session begins. Also consider having the villain recite a short, memorable phrase that you can repeat to kick off the next session, or play a distinctive music track at the end of the cliffhanger session and the beginning of the next one.

Anticipation vs. Disappointment. Cliffhangers create tension through anticipation. The more details the players have before the session ends, the more they can speculate and the lower the dramatic impact. As a tradeoff for withholding information, though, the resolution of the cliffhanger is less likely to be disappointing.

When players have had a week (or more) to imagine the climactic battle about to take place, the real battle has to actually *be* climactic to live up to their expectations. Pausing a session before the PCs enter a room allows their imaginations to run wild, but something really awesome needs to be in the room when they finally do open the door. If you prepare a read-aloud description ahead of time, you'll be able to edit and revise the text until you have something exciting to read to your players.

Less experienced GMs can start by revealing the threat to the PCs and then ending the session. For example, when the PCs stride into the room and see Aleemadra the lich floating near the ceiling surrounded by a strange, shimmering glow, they have more information than if the session ends as the PCs push open the chamber door. This gives the players the opportunity to mull over tactics and share theories without the need to dazzle them when they return to the game.

A memorable dramatic statement from the villain can also set up the next session. For example, if Aleemadra the lich shouts, "Behold, the gate opens!" and a glimmering portal springs up in the center of the room, you arouse both suspense and anticipation—and you can repeat the line before describing the horrible creature that slithers through the portal at the start of the next session.

Following Up. You've done everything right. The players showed up on time, the mat and minis are laid out, you're prepared to pick up where you left off with an extremely cool villain for them to fight. Forty minutes later, the battle is over and you have an eager party ready to continue.

Plan your segue into the next part of the encounter before you're sitting in the GM's chair. The transition can be as simple as, "You cheer in triumph as the lich crumbles to dust. A short time later you've breached the surface and feel the sun's light shining down on you again. You return to town, ready for a well-earned rest." The players can then pick up your thread and begin a period of downtime or learn what you have in mind for their next adventure (see Steve Winter's essay on "Sharpening Your Hooks" for ideas). An enemy who escapes or a witness to the finale who can tell the tale of the party's heroic deed also provides direction for future sessions.

Treasure as Hook. After a titanic battle, PCs might wish to search the area and look for any treasure their enemy left behind. You can keep the excitement going by having them find an unusual bit of treasure or unique item that lays groundwork for the next adventure.

HERE COMES THE TWIST

The party has finally vanquished the evil lich Aleemadra after months of scouring the deepest dungeons for her phylactery. As the players high-five each other, you announce that the PCs found something while searching Aleemadra's treasure chamber. An octagonal amulet, inscribed with the image of a basilisk, lies within a silver coffer. The players stare at each other in shock. The same amulet is worn by Earl Raxright, the man who sent them on the quest to destroy the lich in the first place. What is their connection?

Cliffhangers can be used to introduce new information to the players in a dramatic fashion. When the players learn something that sparks their imagination at the end of a session, it keeps the adventure alive in their minds. As with a postponed battle, the players want to talk about the potential reasons behind this new information and what it will mean for their characters. It also invests the PCs in their next adventure.

Many Cliffs. This type of cliffhanger also has the benefit of being usable multiple times. In the example above, there's no requirement to follow up on the truth behind the basilisk amulet immediately once the next session begins. The PCs might try to investigate the earl and find themselves blocked by his power and position. Other, unrelated adventures could occur before the players find another clue that leads them to the truth behind the dastardly earl.

This mechanism requires you to keep the players' interest by continuing to provide them with new information, not an endless procession of villains who don't contribute anything to the players' knowledge. As a good rule of thumb, have no more than one or two sessions between those that advance a larger plot.

Introducing New Villains. As with Earl Raxright, a cliffhanger can be used to inform the PCs about a new threat or provide a tie between seemingly unconnected characters. These threats might be immediate (such as the famous scene of a defeated villain taking its "final form") or delayed (requiring further action on the PCs' parts). Connecting villains together can illuminate a larger plot in the story, and revealing new ones can provide leads for the next adventure awaiting the PCs.

Reversing Beliefs. A cliffhanger can also provide a twist. The PCs might learn that a beloved NPC has been manipulating them all along. Or that a villain they've been hunting might have good, even noble, reasons for her behavior. The valuable treasure the PCs seek might actually be a dangerous artifact—even more alarming if it's already been delivered into the waiting hands of their patron! This kind of cliffhanger can cause the PCs to reevaluate their objective or can muddy their goals (perhaps spawning the need for more information, and thus more adventures).

UPSETTING THE ORDER

Though twists and turns in the plot can surprise, players usually have an idea of what awaits them during an adventure. Dungeons hold orcs and bugbears guarding piles of shiny treasure; graveyards are full of grasping undead; a dragon's volcano lair contains hordes of elementals and kobold servitors. Occasionally, though, you might want to pull out all the stops and shake up your campaign world. A cliffhanger set right as the status quo changes dramatically can heighten the impact of a dramatic change.

A New World. The PCs have fought for days against the orc hordes of an underground dungeon complex. It seems like forever since they've seen the sun. When they finally defeat the orc chieftain and return to the surface, they're shocked to see a second sun in the sky. What has happened while they've been underground? Pausing at this moment gives the players time to wonder and speculate before the next session begins.

A New Threat. The heroes raced to the temple of the Shield Goddess to replace her sacred artifact in time to prevent a rift to Hell from opening. When they place the artifact on her shrine in the nick of time, they're horrified to find it has no effect. Has the Shield Goddess been imprisoned somehow, or even killed? Was the artifact tainted somehow? The answers will have to wait, as devils already spill forth from tears in reality.

The rise of a new threat right before the end of a session sparks strategizing as well as speculation. Players might wonder if the enemy they now face is a long-term threat or if it can be defeated quickly.

A New Role. A cliffhanger can dramatize change within the party as well. When the players finally uncover Earl Raxright's plan for world destruction and slay him, they won't expect for one of them to be named the new holder of the Basilisk Throne by the grateful people. What will this mean for the player? For the party? Unveiling new titles or powers for the characters right before a session ends adds extra impact to the revelation. So does revealing a previously unknown responsibility of that title or rank: "As the new Earl, you must prepare the grounds for the midsummer tournament and offer a worthy prize to the realm's new champion."

SWITCHING CAMPAIGNS

Campaigns might need to be put on hold for weeks or months while players are unavailable. Vacations, work deadlines, and family commitments can all interrupt regular gameplay. Cliffhangers can be used in these situations to leave the game on a high note while the GM or another player runs a side campaign for a little while.

Related Characters. In a long-running campaign, characters can pick up followers, hirelings, long-lost relatives, or wards that could have adventures of their own. These small adventures can provide more roleplaying material for the players when they return to the main campaign, or plant the seeds for following adventures. For example, if during the secondary adventure a character's cohort is killed, the news could reach the party after the main campaign has resumed and the cliffhanger has resolved. The tension of this out-of-character knowledge keeps the excitement level elevated.

Related Plots. One fun use of a cliffhanger leaves the players at a dramatic moment and then, in the side adventure, provides them with seemingly unrelated pregenerated characters. Only when the players reach the end of this secondary adventure do they realize their characters play an important role in the main campaign. Perhaps the secondary characters discover a valuable artifact that they recognize as a lich's phylactery. When the main heroes resume their battle with Aleemadra the lich, they know they'll also have to track down the phylactery in the hands of their alternates.

Cliffhangers end sessions not with bookkeeping and treasure distribution, but with excitement and mystery. They inflame the players' imaginations with thoughts of what could be coming next in their campaign, and can be a fun way to tease the players with anticipation of the adventure's very next scenes.

An Improv Adventure: The Journey from Here to There

Zeb Cook

In the spirit of doing and not just telling, here is a complete improv adventure intended to give GMs new to the idea a simple story to practice with. This is designed—very loosely—for a party of four to eight low-level characters (no more than about 4th level by *D&D* standards). Of course, since this is meant for improv, it's easy to adjust the number of players, level, or mix of abilities. It is based on sessions run at actual game conventions with groups of players who are frequently strangers to each other. The adventure is meant to be fairly fast playing (completion in about 4 hours or less) and it is not entirely serious, although it is not a farce. The goal is for everyone to have a good time and enjoy a fine adventure—and that's more important than rules precision, power gaming, detailed plots, or earth-shattering stories.

GMs will notice there's no game system called out here, no stat blocks, and no lists of monsters or encounters. This adventure provides a simple framework of setups and possible ways they can be used. To draw the most out of it, GMs should use the rules they are most comfortable with.

The basics of this adventure are very simple. The players start **Here**—a castle or walled town on the edge of the settled lands. They are given a task to deliver a package to **There**—a place several days' journey through the wilderness. That's really all there is to it. It's the traveling from Here to There that makes the adventure.

BEFORE THE ADVENTURE BEGINS

First, make sure to have the crib sheets prepared and ready. This should include the following:

- A selection of low- and mid-level monsters suitable for a wilderness adventure
- A short list of NPC stereotypes: peasants, men-at-arms, tax collectors, nobles, doddering priests, merchants, tavern keepers, and town toughs at a minimum
- The Ten Questions (see the earlier essay, "The Art of Letting Go")

Once everyone has characters and is ready to play, the GM should ask the Questions provide material for encounters to come. Note everyone's answers as best as is practical, and start to identify encounters and themes that will work with the setups in the adventure.

THE START

The characters have all been summoned by the local baron/count/duke/king/priest/boss to do a task for him. Accepting the mission will provide the following benefits (pick one, all, or none):

- Cancel their back taxes
- Gain them favor with the noble
- Get them out of jail
- Provide a handsome reward
- Gain the trust of the local nobility
- Allow them to keep their heads
- Earn points with their deity
- Or whatever else might motivate the characters

The lord's character is not important, so GMs should feel free to create whatever personality they like—arrogant, drunkard, simpering, absent-minded, overworked, or vengeful. Odds are the players will never see the lord again, so his (or her) personality can be whatever works best for the moment. No matter the mood, the lord eventually gives the characters a simple task. He needs a package delivered to the abbot of an old monastery several days' journey through the wilderness. It is a small chest easily carried by one man or mule.

What's in the chest? Of course, the players are instructed not to open the chest. If they do open the package, the GM needs to decide what is inside. Start by listening to the players. They will almost certainly speculate on the contents, and those speculations can be used against them. Suppose, for example, the players decide the chest contains a severed head (don't ask why). After a day or two of traveling, tell them the chest is starting to smell. When they open it (which they almost certainly will), they discover a wheel of stinky cheese, against all their expectations. Why is the lord sending cheese to an abbot? Who knows? Will the players eat the cheese? And what if they arrive without it?

As long as it's not immensely valuable or magical, the chest can hold anything you like: a golden necklace, a mummified hand, a seemingly blank sheet of paper, a book of diplomatic correspondence, a holy icon, or anything else. Odd and mysterious is good, since it provides fuel for player speculation and paranoia.

Frankly, the mission and the task are unimportant. What matters for this adventure is the journey.

SETTING OUT

After negotiating and accepting the task, the players should be encouraged to gather whatever supplies and information they desire. Supplies are no problem, unless they want something exotic or weird. Information will be vague; most of the townsfolk have never ventured far from the town walls. At best, they can point out the road to a village about a day's journey away. A party healer who decides to visit the local temple might be able to acquire useful healing supplies, depending on interaction with the local priest.

Once the characters set out, the adventure is broken down into days. Each day the nature of the land varies and the challenges change. Each day or night includes a unique situation. The rest of the action is driven by simple encounter checks: one for morning travel, one for the afternoon, and three during the night.

DAY 1: ON THE ROAD

The first day takes place in settled lands. The players leave the town and travel on a farm track toward the next village. Small fields and farmsteads along the road gradually grow farther apart as the day wears on.

Make two encounter checks, morning and afternoon. If they indicate an encounter, look at the list of questions and answers for any that seem appropriate to a settled area. Was a player on the run from the law? Afraid of arrest? Send a posse of guards, suspicious of the party, out to check on the group. Did a player want to be rich? Tax collectors stop them to collect the lord's road tax (did he neglect to mention that?). Did someone get clever and say they were afraid of cows? Stampede!

In general, any encounter on the first day should be fairly lightweight. The goal isn't to kill the players at the start of the adventure. The real intent is to show the players how their answers will create the adventure. That will prepare them to react and roleplay the next time a situation reflects their answers.

Also, now is a good time to look for an opportunity to introduce a repeating character or situation: a jealous husband in pursuit of a lothario character, a group of bandits intent on simple robbery. Remember the rules—the setup is everything.

As a complication, the encounter doesn't have to happen immediately. The group of riders could ominously shadow the players for several hours. It might be that they intend no good or they might be honest travelers, more afraid of the characters than the characters are of them.

NIGHT CAMPING

The road leads to a small village, but the characters don't reach it until after dark. Give them the choice to camp or press on to the village in the dark. If they decide to camp, they find a farmer (with his wife and small children) who lets them use his barn for the night. He is probably suspicious of heavily armed strangers showing up at dusk, but he doesn't have the courage to send them away. Roleplay this encounter and see where it goes. Hopefully, the players won't burn the farmstead down. This is often an opportunity to test a player's "best asset" answer or attempt to exercise that skill they never learned.

Assuming the players bed down in the barn, check for encounters during the night (three checks). If any check indicates an encounter, ignore the other results. Since this is nighttime in a settled area, consider using simple robber or small lurking creatures to attack. Again, look at their answers. If a player is embarrassed by the thought of being killed by stirges, now would be a good time to discover the barn is infested with them. Maybe an orc raiding party shows up. Or maybe it's those bandits who were shadowing the group all day.

If a fight breaks out, you can introduce complications such as the farmer and his family trying to ineptly help out or trying to prevent his barn from burning down, keeping the characters' horses from bolting mid-fight, or the fact that the whole structure is rickety and likely to fall down the minute someone slams against a support post.

At any rate, the farmer is going to be unhappy with all the commotion during the night.

THE VILLAGE

If the group presses on, they reach the village in the middle of the night. If the group camps, they reach the village at the end of the next day (after another round of encounter checks while they are on the road). If players complain that the village was supposed to be closer, point out that peasant estimates of time and distance are fungible.

Regardless, the characters arrive at the village at dark/after dark. The village will be silent, with no sign of life. Why?

Again, looking at the player answers (and listening to them as they play), should provide many possible options. For example:

- A character wishes to be seen as noble and honest: The villagers think the characters are bandits come to rob them. They are too terrified to attack, but who knows what will happen if the players let their guard down.

- A character is afraid of werewolves: The villagers are werewolves, of course.

- A character wants to prove his faith: The villagers are demon worshipers and need a suitable sacrifice for tonight's new moon ritual in the parish hall.

Eventually the players will make contact with the villagers. How this is likely to play out depends on above, but possible complications here could include:

- The local dialect makes talking to them extremely difficult.

- They secretly hate the noble the players are working for.

- Those robbers who have been following the party show up and the villagers think the characters are part of the gang.

INTO THE FOREST

After the village, the farm road gradually dwindles to a game track as the group enters forested wilderness that marks the end of civilized settlement. Once again, make two encounter checks during the day. When they camp at night, make note of their precautions and make three encounter checks.

Should the party have an encounter, once again look to their answers for what happens. Creatures listed in the "most embarrassed to be killed by" or "greatest fear" responses are especially useful. If you don't have those precise creatures on hand in your monster list, reskin a stat block or improvise as appropriate. The goal at this point is to push the characters, hurt them (not necessarily kill them), and force them to use spells and magical resources to survive. For the next few encounters, you want them nervous about survival. They might be set upon by orcs, pixies, bandits, ghouls, or anything else that threatens the group. These can be relatively straight up fights, although players should be encouraged to react to their characters' fears and embarrassments appropriately.

THE RIVER CROSSING

At midday, the party approaches an obstacle. A broad-flowing river blocks their progress. The shores are wooded on both sides, but the far bank appears to have an old rotting ferry landing. Searching this side reveals no other crossing point. The group must find a way across.

The river is about 200 feet across and appears to have a strong but swimmable current. Nothing indicates the depth of the water. No apparent creatures lurk on the opposite bank.

There are three basic ways to cross, although players might come up with others.

- Everybody swims across. Of course, if anyone noted they never learned how to swim, that might be a problem.

- The group has enough rope that someone could swim across and fasten a line on the far bank so everyone else can cross safely.

- Spend a lot of time—a day—building a crude raft and trying to pole across.

In any case, the crossing is not as simple as that. Waiting for the party (or the lone swimmer) is an automatic encounter with something hostile— ideally something someone has already mentioned. It might be a giant alligator, an undead octopus, nixies, a drowned zombie boatman, or other local hazard.

Furthermore, the fight has complications. The monster will be hidden (underwater or in the woods) until the target is close. Second, the current is strong. A lone swimmer can't stop swimming until they get to shore— and then they might still have 200 feet of wet rope attached to them. Let the first swimmer just reach the shore before springing the trap. As for rafts, they tip over easily and most of the party will have to keep paddling or poling to get across.

The encounter should have both elements of comedy and tragedy. One character trying to fight a zombie while dragging 200 feet of rope as his friends hold the other end could be hysterical or fatal, depending on circumstances. A whole party on a makeshift raft attacked by nixies isn't likely to end well. While the GM should not engineer a total party kill, death or serious injury should be a possibility.

THE MONASTERY

For the characters who survive the river crossing, the rest of the day should pass quietly. The party emerges from the woods and can once again pick up the trail. By the end of the day, the monastery is in sight.

The place is a simple motte-and-bailey structure set in a treeless vale. A dry ditch surrounds the wooden stockade. Inside are several simple buildings—storehouses and a kitchen. At the back of the stockade stands a small hill with a two-story tower on top of it. Characters spot a main gate and smaller gate toward the rear of the stockade. This might be a monastery, but these monks are not fools.

At this point the GM should take a few moments to look at the "last thing I want to meet on a dark night" answers for inspiration. This can provide a final villain for the adventure. If a player said "vampire," then a vampire has moved into the tower and most of the monks are dead (or undead). If a player said "dragon," then a dragon (age level depending on the party strength) has chosen the monastery as its lair. Most of the monks are dead, though a few survivors might give panicked reports to the characters. If the player said "lich"—something too strong for a low-level party—then they discover the abbot is secretly a mage ransacking the libraries in search of the secret to lichdom. Of course, his monks are charmed to protect and serve him.

Whatever its nature, the foe should be challenging; not an impossible encounter, but an enemy that require skills, teamwork, and maybe a little bit of luck to bring down. Characters could easily die, but unless they all blunder badly at least one should survive to tell the tale. The goal is excitement and drama, not necessarily the death of all involved.

Once the main boss is determined, choose minions appropriate for the foe. These should be fairly basic but numerous, certainly enough to keep everyone from concentrating on the boss. Also look at the "remembered as" and "awesome things" questions for inspiration on how to make the fight heroic. If a player wants to be remembered as gallant and brave, give him opportunities to play the role during the fight. If giant meteor fireballs would be awesome, maybe the monks were making fireworks for the birthday of the noble who sent you here. (It would be awesome if they caught on fire.)

Depending on the nature of the final encounter, the monastery will either be dark and silent or eerily lit by the invaders. Neither option should look normal to encourage players to be cautious. The walls are simple for a thief to climb and can be scaled by others with a little effort. Once they're safely inside, give the characters a chance to discover clues about the nature of their foe(s). They can even be rewarded with minor magic to help them through the finale.

At this stage, don't make things too difficult for the players. The goal is to reach to the final fight while building tension as they go. If the monastery has been taken over by an evil mage and his orc allies, make it possible to sneak through—or almost through—the orc camp without raising the alarm. Let them to get to that final fight on a knife's edge feeling that a small mistake could bring everything crashing down. Tempt individual players with their life's ambition, such as finding a room full of gold or the bodies of murdered monks who *must* be avenged.

Once the final fight starts, keep the pace moving quickly. Throw in threats from unexpected directions (the orcs in the camp wake up and rush toward the tower). Use the players' hopes and fears to make the encounter feel epic and dangerous. Characters can die, although there should always be at least a few who flee or stagger out triumphant at the end.

With a little preparation and practice, improvisational gaming can be a great GM's tool. All the principles and structure given here can be applied to almost any type of adventure situation. All it takes is a little fearlessness and trust on the part of the GM and the players. It can look challenging for those who have never tried this method before, but a good session is inspiring, rewarding the GM with new skills and confidence and the players with adventures they didn't just play but helped create.

Finally, always remember the last rule of improv: *Have fun!*

MAKE YOUR GAME YOUR OWN!

Let the Kobolds show you the way with the award-winning series of Kobold Guides covering every aspect of game design and game play.

CPSIA information can be obtained
at www.ICGtesting.com
Printed in the USA
BVHW04s0217220618
519732BV00018B/319/P